Jack the Ripper

A Scientific Analysis

Francis E Westfield B.Sc. (Hons), P.G.C.E

Contents

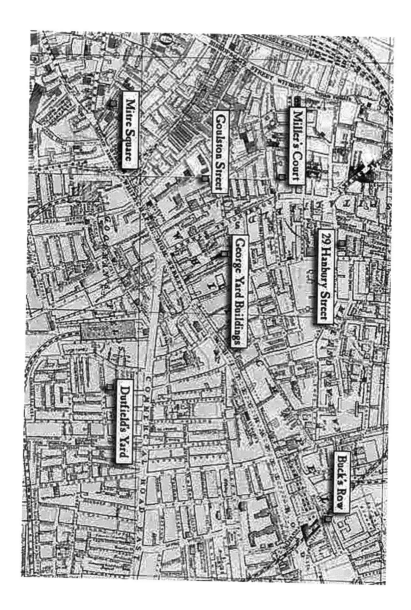

Mitre Square

Goulston Street

Miller's Court

29 Hanbury Street

George Yard Buildings

Dutfield's Yard

Buck's Row

Chapter 1

An overview of the crime scene 1888

First in 1888 look at the crime scene map above assume it to be A4 size then my analysis below has meaning.

Jack the ripper is on many G.C.S.E. specifications (syllabuses) in England and is still very much alive, though anonymous, in the collective public consciousness. The first British serial killer was never identified and caught at the time can we do better now?

Before my introduction let us get a handle on the geography in this small area of East London.

On the map (dotted with incident scenes) let us start by visualising the relationship between the crime scenes:

Miller's Court was where Mary Kelly was found.

Goulston street where (above the piece of Catherine Eddowes' apron) the graffito showing rivalry between two police forces was written and washed off later by police thinking it would inflame the Jewish community.

The Metropolitan police force (Scotland Yard) and the jurisdiction of the City of London Police (old Jewry police as their nickname was at the time) were in charge depending on where the bodies were found.

"The Juwes are not the men that will not be blamed for nothing"

in chalk writing, was found on the wall of Wentworth Model Dwellings and was washed off so as not to offend Jewish people or members of the Craft. This writing had in fact nothing to do with these sections of the population, it was a statement by a City of London Old Jewry policeman not wanting his force to being blamed for not clearing up the murders (the writing was after all in Met. Territory). The name came from the Old Jewry Police Headquarters of the city police and had therefore nothing to do with Jews or the Jewish race.

The above attribution to anti-semitic nonsense was therefore nothing of the sort but a reference to two competing police forces in the area, one of which did not wish to be blamed for not locating and identifying the killer.

» Mitre Square where Catherine Eddowes body was found.

» 29 Hanbury Street where Anne Chapman's body lay.

» The George Yard Buildings where Martha Tabram was found.

» Dutfield's Yard where the body of Liz Stride was located.

» Finally Buck's Row where Polly Nichols' body was found.

Working from left to right across the map geographically not chronologically. If we number them one to seven then in chronological order it would read:

One in the middle of the map, two top right, three middle top, four bottom right, five bottom left, six middle left and seven top left.

Assuming Martha Tabram's murder to be the first then my analysis of an A4 size version of this is as follows:

I took a ruler and measured the distance in cm. between each murder site and the next and found (as the crow flies) a distance of 16.03 between the first and second sites, 15.75 between the second and third sites. 16.00 CM between the third and fourth sites. 16.02 was the distance between the fourth and fifth sites. 11.5 was the distance between sites 5 and 7, ignoring the Goulston Street graffito. I took the average (11.854 CM) and used it as a radius around each site. Where the radii intersected I recorded two common sites. One intersection just north of George Yard buildings and the other just north east of the east end of Whitechapel High Street. This could indicate that the murderer changed addresses during the spree (as did Joseph Barnett) or could just be a red herring. Note the astonishing first four distance measurements. A very consistent distance travelled. Is this an indication of someone being comfortable within their own geographical area or coincidental or because

I plotted and measured as the crow flies? Another suggestion is that the Ripper just followed the women home after pub closing time.

After my geographical crime scene pattern analysis let us return to the background, events and suspect trail and try to eliminate all but the Ripper from the scene.

Chapter 2

The unknown Jack the Ripper and social scene.

All the killings took place within one square mile in the East end and the city of London surrounding Whitechapel in a ten week spree in 1888.

Nine hundred thousand people lived in slum-like conditions in this area. Rubbish and raw sewage littered and coated the streets. This gave the streets a disgusting odour. Some constables made sanitary inspections but it changed little. Cattle and sheep were herded through the streets to slaughterhouses close by.

There were many lodging houses with several large families crammed together. Standing taps outside some properties were used to collect water to wash in or wash clothes. Women tried to earn a little by tailoring jobs but some were forced onto the streets to make ends meet if their husbands had no work (or to supplement their income).

The name Whitechapel derived from the stone walls of the chapel of Ease of St. Mary Matfelon which were white. This church, (before it was damaged in the air raids of 1940 and pulled down in 1952) was a fixture of Whitechapel Road.

Spitalfields, situated immediately north of Whitechapel, was once the hub of the silk weaving industry, but by 1888 this industry had long died out and there were few opportunities for employment in the area. Many houses had been altered from empty former homes of wealthy families to form 'Doss' houses. This was where people could get shelter for a few pennies per night. Whole families could procure a room for eight pennies per night. Meals at that time would cost about one penny three farthings each. It was against this backdrop that the crimes took place. Several gangs would try to extort money using intimidation. Through this social squalor, intimidation and grinding poverty the Ripper started his serial killing spree.

The female victims were prostitutes (who were also known as unfortunates) and would go with a client up an alley for as little as four pennies, or two shillings for a whole evening, such was the poverty in the area at that time. London's Metropolitan Police Service estimated that in 1888 there were approximately 1200 prostitutes and 62 brothels in Whitechapel alone.

In the mid nineteenth century there was an influx of Irish immigrants and from 1882 Jewish refugees from Eastern Europe and Tsarist Russia moved into the same area. The area thus became very crowded and work and housing conditions worsened boosting the development of a significant economic underclass. Robbery, violence (there was at least one gang in the East end at that time, the white's Row gang in Spitalfields) and alcohol dependency were omnipresent.

The bodies were found in the main regions of Whitechapel, Spitalfields, Aldgate and the city of London proper. The victims were: Mary Ann Nichols 31.8.1888, Eliza Anne Chapman 8.9.1888, Liz Stride 30.9.1888, Catherine Eddowes (Kate) 30.9.1888 and Mary Jane Kelly 9.11.1888. Eleven women were murdered in the East end area between the 3rd of April 1888 and the 13th of February 1891. They were gathered into a single file, referred to in the police docket as the Whitechapel murders. However most authors and theorists adhere to the canonical five listed above. Some claim Martha Tabram killed on the 7th Aug 1888 and Alice McKenzie killed on the 17th July 1889 as extra first and last victims too.

For a full list of victims, together with alternative spellings and aliases, see Chapter 3.

According to the FBI a murderer who kills more than three times is a 'serial killer'. Having analysed many patterns associated with serial killers the FBI also point out that serial killers, like the

Ripper, never leave clues at the scene of the crime. This was the same pattern exhibited in the Ripper case apart from a possible torn envelope. (*See Later - Page: 128*).

The Dorset Street and Whitechapel areas seem to indicate the most likely places for the residence of Jack the Ripper (this is according to data received from one group using modern geographical profiling) however using the same techniques another team suggests the killer may have lived at or immediately around Flower and Dean Street in East London.

He was called Jack the Ripper after the 'Dear Boss' letter to the Central News Agency received on September 27th 1888—this was signed "Yours truly, Jack the Ripper".

The Saucy Jack written communication is also accepted as genuine as the Dear Boss letter.

The From Hell letter may be a third communication that will stand up to analysis (although some people, over the years, have claimed it was the boss of the Central News Agency who forged the letters to boost circulation figures.).

Over three hundred letters were sent to the central news agency and individual newspapers, at that time, asserting that they were Jack the Ripper. Only the three cited above seem to be genuine. He may have been left handed as some of the victims were obviously cut from left to right as we look at the body. It could have been a right handed individual approaching from behind since prostitute anal sex was common then.

Some of the prostitutes were known as bangtails (see the From Hell film (2001) starring Jonny Deppe) for taking sex from behind which would explain this. However in a recent (2009) crime CSI Las Vegas television episode, who have their own forensic advisor, the pathologist in the mortuary stated "Most doctors say you cannot prove handedness from knife wounds".

Another scenario, unlikely in the case of Jack the Ripper, is that the murderer feigns right / left handedness or being ambidextrous, to foil the investigation.

In a related line of research a graphologist looking at the Dear Boss letter concluded he was disturbed.

In Catherine Eddowes case he took part of her blood-soaked apron but dropped it a quarter of a mile from the scene towards the east end of London—on his way home perhaps? Was it, however, simply a rag used as a sanitary towel (which was typical of that time), made from the same type of material (or the woman ran out of rags)?

Over the years more than 200 suspects have been suggested for the self-styled Jack the Ripper. I intend to find as many suspects as possible and analyse the evidence for each one.

Being an ex-scientist and science teacher I will try to add occasional scientific approaches to help move things forward.

Three things make this difficult.

Firstly, the established suspects list may not contain the real Jack the Ripper.

Secondly, names are forever changing in spelling and multiple names can be found for individuals, either to hide crimes or they have changed their names or are known by several names or are poorly reported, recorded or combinations of these. E.g. Kosminski, as you will find out, has several different Christian names and at least one alias.

Nicknames do not help either—Leather Apron applies to several suspects as does Polish/Jew.

Thirdly this was before basic forensics became established. Even fingerprinting was not available, although it was being devised by Francis Galton at the time who was searching for a scientific basis, and trying to elucidate the probability of two people having the same prints. It had been introduced in the 1860's by Sir William James Herschel in India and their potential use in forensic work was first proposed by Dr. Henry Faulds in 1880.

In 1892 Argentinian police researcher Juan Vucetich developed a classification system for digit prints which was used in Latin America. This same system came into use in Europe and North America in 1806, pioneered by Sir Edward Richard Henry.

Fingerprinting was introduced to Scotland Yard in 1902.

A year before that Dr. Paul Uhlenhuth founded a method of testing blood stains to determine if they were Human in origin.

Apart from the person who became my favourite suspect, Joe Barnett (the paramour of the last victim) there is no reason, except for order and to keep count, in the number system I will use. I will also check to see which suspects were in Jail or have alibis for any or all of the murders.

A general description, for the Ripper would be, a man aged between 25 and 35, about 5' 6" tall, with blue eyes and of stocky build with a downturned black moustache, possibly wearing a bowler hat and left handed.

Also a long thin amputation knife was said to have been used in the crimes (it has been suggested, again in the film From Hell, that it could have been a Liston knife, named for Robert Liston who used similar knives at a very fast rate to reduce suffering, whilst amputating limbs, in the days before anaesthetics).

Fingerprinting was not used to solve a murder until nine years later, in India.

Four years after that Scotland Yard started using fingerprinting on a regular basis. Until then they would have to rely on witness statements, catching someone in the act or patterns of behaviour being repeated and general descriptions of the miscreants.

The number of victims is an enigma in itself. Were there five victims officially? Sir Melville MacNaghten stated "the Whitechapel murderer had five victims and five victims only". However, according to Dr. Percy Clark, the assistant to the examining pathologist, he found that only three of the victim's injuries conformed to the same pattern, and he suggested that the other murders were by copy cat killers.

Some authors believe there were 11 murders starting or ending in America and carried out by a well-travelled sailor.

The case was closed in 1892 but that does not stop the research. I had been interested in the Jack the Ripper events for some years and with the advent of the internet (search engines and podcasts) I found that my research could proceed apace.

Here are my motives for writing this tome. No one, as far as I can ascertain, has produced a scientific evaluation of all the suspects suggested over the 127 years since the Whitechapel murders took place.

It seemed to me that in 2011 ; with the availability of the internet, many books have been published on this subject (over 160), past and present newspaper articles, new evidence from Scotland Yard and released files, together with the original photographic, inquest and coroner's reports, a more comprehensive analysis of each suspect could be carried out.

The crime scenes and a little of the background of each murder should also provide additional data which could point towards one or more of the suspects as being Jack the Ripper. The name Jack the Ripper may have come from a letter to Scotland Yard from a drunken journalist called Thomas Bulling pretending to be a killer of that nom de plume. That does not preclude the existence of the serial killer as some would have one believe.

By the time the last one occurred the police were in the new habit of securing the crime scene (even if it was only to send in the bloodhounds, Bruno and Burgho to sniff out the killer). Even though the hounds never arrived (when they were being trained in Surrey they apparently bolted and were never seen again) the evidence was preserved for a basic analysis.

Another story about the bloodhounds comes from retired policeman Paul Harrison who claimed that they had been returned to their owner in Scarborough. In an article in the Croyden Advertiser dated Saturday October 13th 1888 it is claimed that demonstrations of two bloodhounds in action, tracing strangers had taken place before Sir Charles Warren. These dogs were called Burgho and Barnaby.

However, there is always the chance that the suspect has never been identified and that books and articles have errors e.g. mixing up suspects, which was already evident to me having read two works by authors on the subject before I started this project.

Inspector F.G. Abberline was drafted in from H division to help co-ordinate inquires as he had good local geographical knowledge. The police at the time interviewed over 2000 people, over 300 were further investigated and 80 people were detained. Yet they could not finger the actual killer. Just in case a certain type of individual was involved, 76 butchers and slaughterers were investigated covering all their employees for the past six months as well. However, employing as much scientific curiosity together with rigorous testing of theories using Popper's principle of falsification I will endeavour to intensify the evidence to build a major suspect profile and eliminate, using evidence, as many of the other suspects from the scene as I can.

Even today, 127 years later, the Whitechapel murders and the identity of Jack the Ripper can fascinate us and interest each new generation hungry for details that are new or unusual. Most authors detail only between 5 and 10 suspect candidates (usually based on the accepted original official police suspects to quickly eliminate all but one (their pet theory) and then set about elaborating their theory to give it substance and apparent value. I, however, will take all available suspects as a starting point and will try to eliminate each one until a single promising candidate remains or one suspect collects many supporting pieces of information making an apparently strong case.

His modus operandi (referred to as M.O. from now on) was not fully understood until a few years ago and seems to be; the victim and the Ripper faced each other. When she lifted her skirts to perform a sex act with the client her hands were occupied and she was effectively defenceless. Or the other way round, (with anal sex being used as a method of contraception in those days) raising the skirt and undergarments from behind, the hands would still be occupied and he could have strangled her from behind.

The woman would have been seized by the throat and strangled until she put up no more resistance. Then he would lower the victim to the ground with her head to his left cutting the woman's throat while she was on the ground.

Evidence from splatter stains indicate the blood having pooled beside or under the neck and head of the victim rather than the front (where it would have flowed from if they had been standing). If he reached over from the victim's right side to cut the left side of her throat, the blood flow would have been directed away from him. Then he made mutilations standing over the body, collected an appropriate trophy (some suggest held between his shirt and tie others suggest in his black bag or Gladstone doctor's bag) and left.

A link to bloodstained ties will be made later on. Links to bloodstained cuffs and shirts will also be shown in connection with several subjects in due course.

Forget notions of a thick pea soup type fog—it only happened in October that year (understandably, there were no Ripper murders in that month), and a cloaked, tall individual with a top hat and shiny black bag. Jack the Ripper was no mystical and mysterious person. He was a killer with a coherent plan.

On 17th March 2005 an internet file was published by Robert Keppel and Joseph Weis after the analysis of similar crimes comparing 3358 homicides from 1981-95 from Washington State's database and they concluded that the signature from the Jack the Ripper killings was very rare. They cited the combination of Ripper traits as; picquerism, overkill, incapacitation, domination and control, open and displayed, unusual body position, sexual degradation, mutilation, organ harvesting, specific areas of attack, preplanning and organization and a combination of signature features.

All weather reports for the dates of the killings indicate nothing more sinister than a one hour thunder storm between two and three p.m. on Thursday the 30th of August 1888 close to the Mary Ann Nichols murder. No romantic yet sinister dense London fog seen in media portrayals. The killer did not wear a cloak or carry a black shiny surgical equipment laden doctor's Gladstone bag. A coat yes, a scarf perhaps and a hat which might have been of the deerstalker variety would be more accurate which can be gleaned from the three reliable witness statements throughout the course of the killing spree.

In 1912 in Lloyd's Weekly News Detective Inspector Edmund Reid stated;

"Here are the only known facts. The whole of the murders were done after the public houses were closed; all were killed in the same manner. That is all we know for certain. My opinion is that the perpetrator of the crimes was a man who was in the habit of using a certain public-house, and of remaining there until closing time. Leaving with the rest of the customers, with what soldiers call 'a touch of delirium triangle,' he would leave with one of the women. My belief is that he would in some dark corner attack her with the knife and cut her up. Having satisfied his maniacal blood-lust he would go away home, and the next day know nothing about it. One thing to my mind is quite certain, and that is that he lived in the district".

The list of all 200 suspects (that I can find) suggested in the media since 1888 follows later with, in some cases, a photograph of the suspect and a short description of his or her biography.

For each I will give a potted summary of their occupations, addresses, ages, heights, habits, M.O. and why they were considered.

I will also supply some analysis, credit any author who first proposed them as a suspect and indicate why they could or could not be Jack the Ripper.

Only one will be highlighted and the evidence for him being the ripper will be detailed *(Page 129)* (as used in one of the ripper letters).

Wikipedia has subdivided the types of suspects as follows:

A Contemporary police opinion which included, Druitt, Chapman, Kosminski, Ostrog, Pizer, Sadler and Tumblety.

B. Contemporary press and public opinion suggesting, Bury, Cream, Cutbush, Deeming, Feigenbaum and D'Onston Stephenson and

C. Opinions by later authors highlighting, Barnett, Carroll, Cohen, Gull, Hutchinson, Kelly, Maybrick, Pedachenko, Blavatsky, Sickert, Silver, Stephen, Thompson, Prince Albert Victor and Sir. John Williams.

There was a general pattern associated with the victims. Most were between the ages of 39 and 47. They were locally resident in the East End of London. Most were engaged in prostitution. Many were habitual drunks and all were estranged from their husbands and families.

Ironically it was pointed out by George Bernard Shaw that the "gruesome murders succeeded where social reformers had failed by managing to attract widespread attention to the area's conditions". (According to Time Magazine).

There now follows a list of the victims and suspects.

I will then detail the crimes, victim's photographs and letters, one death certificate, (Mary Kelly's) and what the crime scenes look like now.

Chapter 3

Full List of Murder Victims in Chronological Order of Deaths.

Emma Jackson

The body of 28 year old prostitute Emma Jackson was found in a brothel in St.Giles, central London, in April 1863. She had not been robbed and had sustained five wounds to her throat.

Harriet Buswell

Was found with her throat slashed at her lodgings in Great Coram Street after returning there with a male guest the evening before. This was on the 25th of December 1872.

Emma Elizabeth Smith

Aged 45 murdered on 3rd April 1888.

Martha Tabram (alias Turner)

Aged 35-40 murdered on 7th Aug 1888.

Mary Ann Nichols

Murdered on 31st August 1888.

Annie Siffey (alias Chapman)

Murdered on 8th Sept 1888.

Elizabeth Stride

Murdered on 29th Sept 1888.

Catherine Eddowes (Kate)

Murdered on 29th Sept 1888.

Marie Jeanette Kelly
(a.k.a. Black Mary / Fair Emma / Mary Jane Kelly)

Murdered on 9.11.1888.

Rose Mylett alias Lizzie Davis.
(A.k.a. Fair Clara, Catherine Millett, Alice Downey Downe and Elizabeth Davis, Alice.)

Murdered on 20.12.1888

Her body was found on Thursday at 4.15 a.m. in Clarke's yard off Poplar High Street.

Although the police believed she had just choked to death on her own vomit the police surgeons came to the conclusion that she had been strangled with a ligature. There were no recorded mutilations of the body. Therefore a tenuous link to the Ripper.

Alice McKenzie
(a.k.a. "clay pipe Alice" and Alice Bryant)

Murdered on 17th July 1889. At 12.50 a.m.

Police Constable Andrews found the body of a woman lying on the pavement in Castle Alley. Blood flowed from two stab wounds to the neck and her skirts had been raised showing blood across her abdomen, which had also been mutilated. A cut was made from left to right and there was a seven inch wound from her left breast to her navel. One coroner thought it like the Ripper murders and another did not, whereas the police (Monro who was on duty while Anderson was on leave) believed it was identical with the Ripper's M.O.

Torso of female.

Found on 10th Sept.1889.

Frances Coles

(a.k.a. Frances Coleman, Frances Hawkins and 'Carroty Nell')

Murdered on 13th Feb 1891 a t 2.15 a.m.

P.C. Ernest Thompson found the body at the corner of Swallow Gardens and Chamber Street. Blood was flowing from her throat and he saw her blink one eye. He had to stay with the body, as she was still alive, yet he heard footfalls retreating from the scene. His inability to follow what could have been the Ripper. This fact is said to have haunted him for the rest of his days. The neck wounds were consistent with her head being held back (possibly with the left hand) while cutting with the right.

The Main Victims and What Happened to Them

Mary Ann Nichols

At 3.40 a.m. on Friday 31st August 1888, Charles Cross, on his way to work discovered Nichols body as he turned into Bucks row from its eastern entrance off Brady street on his way to Pickfords on City Road.

The examination of the body, after it had been taken to the morgue and had the clothes removed and been washed down, showed not only a deep gash across the neck as was observed outside, but that the body had been disembowelled. There was a deep, jagged knife injury on the left lower abdomen. Three or four cuts, violently inflicted were observed on the right hand side of the lower abdomen. There were several incisions running across the abdomen. The injuries were from left to right and may have been carried out by a left-handed person. All the injuries had been caused by the same instrument.

A piece of broken mirror was the most valuable of her possessions found with the body. This was paraphrased from the inquest testimony reported in the Times newspaper. According to the Echo dated 1.9.1888 the "high-rip gang" were first suspected by the police then some officers assumed a maniac had committed the crime. It was soon realised that this was no ordinary murder.

Eliza Ann Chapman.

At 29 Hanbury street, Spitalfields at 5.45 a.m. John Davis, a resident, went out of his first floor flat to the tap at the other end of the yard to throw water on his face after dressing. He walked along the passage to the tap, pulled the rear yard door open and saw Chapman's body. Her throat was cut deeply from left and back all the way round. Her legs were pulled up and her abdomen opened with intestines visible. Some of her intestines were placed over her right shoulder.

There are perhaps six reasons for removing the entrails. First, to shock, making bigger headlines for one who collected cuttings as some serial killers do. A second reason is the old idea of predicting events using entrails. The third reason could link us with freemasonry rituals. The fourth reason could have involved a practical motive. It would have been easier to find the uterus at the bottom of the abdominal cavity and the kidneys at the back. A fifth reason is that it could have been a random act of violence and the sixth reason could have involved perverse curiosity.

There was a large quantity of blood and the stomach was over the left shoulder. Oddly various possessions were arranged near the railing. They included: a small piece of coarse muslin, a small-tooth comb and a pocket comb in a paper case.

Elizabeth Stride.

The first of the two victims killed on the same night was found in Berner Street off the Commercial Road. Berner Street is now known as Henriques Street and is a narrow street leading in a North to South direction off Commercial Road, Whitechapel. This was the night of the 30th September 1888.

At around 1 a.m. Louis Diemschutz turned his pony and trap into Dutfields yard. He was returning from a market at Crystal Palace where he had been selling some cheap jewellery which he made. His pony appeared to shy away from something and pulled to the left. He realised that it was a woman's body. He and an associate, after seeing the body by match light, got a nearby constable Henry Lamb. Her throat had been cut through the windpipe releasing a large amount of blood.

Dr Fred William Blackwell reported:

"She was lying on her left side obliquely across the passage, her face looking towards the right wall. Her legs were drawn up. All parts of the body were warm except the hands. The right hand was opened and on the chest and smeared with blood. The left hand was partly closed and was lying on the ground containing a small packet of cachous wrapped in tissue paper. The silk scarf round her neck had been pulled very tight. There was a long incision in the neck which exactly corresponded with the lower border of the scarf. The blood was running down the gutter into the drain in the opposite direction from the feet. There was about one pound weight of clotted blood close by the body."

Some researchers, for example Trevor Marriott, believe that 'Long Liz' Stride does not fit the overall pattern of the murders ascribed to the Ripper. He has also suggested, in a podcast, that the killer might not have returned to an address in Whitechapel after each murder and that slipping in amongst the moving people on main roads through the area (and ultimately out of it) would be more likely.

Catherine Eddowes (Kate).

Many sources claim Catherine Eddowes knew of Jack the Ripper's identity before he came to murder her. Why did she not go to the police with her suspicions?

Catherine Eddowes was the victim of the second murder committed in Mitre Square on the evening of 30th Sept.

At 1.44 a.m. Edward Watkins shone his bull lamp into Mitre square, Aldgate (Old Gate) and saw the body of a woman he described as 'being ripped up like a pig'. Her clothes had been drawn up above the abdomen and both thighs were naked. A thimble was lying off the finger on the right side. The abdomen was exposed and there was terrible mutilation to the face. With V shapes cut into each cheek, a slice taken from the nose (syphilis was common among prostitutes and their clients this could indicate you gave me that disease so I cut your nose off) and cuts across both eyelids (the eyes being the key to the soul or organs capable of deception, perhaps). The throat had been cut straight across and the intestines pulled out and placed over the right shoulder and smeared with excrement. The lobe and auricle of the left ear was cut obliquely through and not removed as the press later suggested. One of her kidneys had been excised and removed.

Later a box was sent to the leader of the Vigilance committee containing one half of a human kidney. The other half, it was claimed by the author of the letter attached, he had fried and eaten. The last part of the note stated "catch me when you can Mister Lushk". Was it a hoax using any old kidney or her kidney half, sent by J.T.R. himself? In the view of Dr.Openshaw (the pathology curator of the London Hospital) it was a Human kidney cut longitudinally and it came from an adult. He also stated that he thought it to be the left kidney (Eddowes's left kidney was missing). Some reports also stated that a portion of the renal artery was attached, yet others who examined the kidney said that it had been trimmed down. Her swollen tongue indicated strangulation as the cause of death.

Mary Jeanette Kelly.

She was the only victim whom the police photographed at the scene of the crime.

Joe Barnett and Mary Kelly's room (where the murder of Kelly took place) was at 13 Miller's Court, Dorset Street and was a single room,(10' x 12'). It was in reality a partitioned section of the ground floor back room of the main house. The only door was just inside the arched entry to the court (as reported by The Viper in the website casebook: Jack the Ripper).

Thomas Bowyer was sent to collect 29s. rental arrears from her on the morning of Friday 9th November 1888. He looked through her broken window (at 10.30 a.m.) drew back the old muslin curtain and saw a horrific scene. Blood covered the floor and the bed and Kelly's entrails were scattered round the room.

He and his boss ran to Commercial Street Police Station and informed Inspector Beck of their discovery.

At 1.30 p.m. Superintendent Arnold had the window removed to let a photographer climb inside to take photographs of the body in situ. Then after the photographer climbed out, the door was broken in by an axe (actually broken open with a pickaxe according to a contemporary drawing of the scene outside number 13 Millers court, Dorset Street). Various organs had been placed, with care, on a bedside table; skin from the thighs and rest of the legs, breasts and her nose. Her liver was found between her feet. Neatly placed on a chair on the other side of the room were the dead woman's clothes (except for an undergarment with puffed sleeves which she had been wearing). A man's pipe was found on the mantelpiece (later shown to belong to Joseph Barnett). Stale bread was found in the cupboard as well as a number of ginger beer bottles.

Ironically a poster offering a £100 reward for information leading to the arrest of Jack the Ripper was placed immediately opposite Mary Kelly's room.

Two surgeons were given the job of taking the torso and body parts in two bags to the mortuary. Although in addition, as stated by author Donald Rumbelow (paraphrasing) "the main body was placed under a cloth and a scratched and dirty coffin was arranged to take the corpse away as crows of people, curious to gain a first hand impression of the Ripper's work assembled."

The heart had been removed from the pericardium through a hole made below the organ.

The autopsy was at 2.p.m. Rigor mortis had started and was reaching its peak (about 3 p.m.) during the examination, indicating 12 hours since the murder, suggesting that Kelly died at approximately 3.30 a.m. (However a witness claimed that they saw the victim at 8.30a.m.). Rigor mortis may not have fully set in and the heat in the room may have put off the time of death determination by hours.

Years later in a handwritten series of numbered notes Sir Melville L. Macnachten (who probably transcribed / edited them from Abberline's reports) suggested two hours for the Kelly murder. Presumably 8.30 to 10.30 a.m. Macnachten did not join Scotland Yard until 1894 so had no first hand experience of the Whitechapel murders.

This scene elicits several interesting questions:

Why were most of her clothes neatly placed on a chair when blood and skin and guts were thrown round?

Why was she naked and the door locked?

With a poster warning her about Jack the Ripper so near by, how did someone get into her flat?

Who locked the flat? Not even the landlord had a spare key—the door had to be broken down by his assistant. Were the spare keys given to Joseph Barnett and Joseph Fleming?

Did someone pay her to get undressed as a prelude to sex? Was it someone she knew or was she just drunk or both?

Why were the organs placed in order on the bedside table when blood, skin and guts were strewn round the room? Was it Dr. Tumblety looking for a womb, and this time had the space, light and time to do it? Yet only the heart was taken.

Tumblety, who had an obsession with uteri and collected them would not have left that. This was after the murderer had taken the time to arrange the organs on the bedside table, so in my opinion Dr. Tumblety could never have murdered Kelly, therefore he is not Jack the Ripper.

This makes the case all the stronger for Barnett or the Polish / Jew Kominski. The lamp was extinguished and on its side but that did not matter as a fierce fire had been burning in the grate and some of her clothes had been used to fuel the fire. Evidence of two clay pipes were in the ashes. The reason for using clay pipes, instead of wood pipes resided not only in their cheaper cost but also if you roast them in a fire you burn the goo off and kill bacteria. This was a regular event in earlier London coffee houses, leaving the pipes in the grate for use of patrons the next day.

The kettle had not only boiled dry but the spout had fallen off due to the solder having melted. Such an intense, bright fire can provide enough light for the murderer to work his bloody deeds. It can also be used to burn off blood stained clothes and cloths used to wash blood off hands.

She was singing about violets at 2a.m. and had brought a man back to her room (she never brought clients back therefore it was most probably Joe Barnett). At 4a.m. a faint cry of murder was heard, but ignored. Dorset Street was a violent place and drunken scuffles were commonplace.

At 7.30 a.m. Catherine Pickett, a flower seller who lived in Miller's court, went to Kelly's room in order to borrow something but got no reply.

Various suggestions have surfaced in recent years that her left femur was cut by a hatchet or axe.

Various authors have spotted the letters FM scratched on the wall near the bed, some have suggested in blood (splatter) others have recorded a scratched set of initials either by the killer or by the occupant. Perhaps Simon Owen in the 1980's spotted this first. Assuming the scratches to be real we could deduce: free-mason / fish money / Fool's money / find money / Florence Maybrick? / fanny money / f--- money / freedom money(i.e. to get back to Ireland / find money / free money / free me. / find mate / fools marry / factor money (i.e. rent money) / friend Maria i.e. Maria Harvey a laundress living at 3 New Court off Dorset Street, who stayed with Mary Kelly on both the Monday & Tuesday before her death or the Fate of Martha Tabram to be read to her again by Barnett. All or nothing in this instance as the letters are disputed.

Police photograph of Mary Kelly's corpse taken from the direction of the muslin curtain broken window and previously bolted and locked door. Horrific injuries included the breasts removed, the abdomen eviscerated and the heart removed. Skin and flesh, down to the bone, from the thighs also removed. The nose was cut off and the left hand placed in the abdominal cavity. The puffed shoulder undergarment is clearly visible (although missed by several authors who had the picture on display in their books) but the rest of the clothes were placed neatly on a chair. The uterus, one breast and kidney were under the head. The other breast had been placed at her right foot. The liver was found between her feet. The heart had been removed downwards through the pericardial sac and away from the apartment. The head had been positioned facing left towards the door (for initial shock value?). Another suggestion is that her head was displaced due to the uterus placed under it indicating that the killer wished to point out that she let her head rule that part of her body and not her heart.

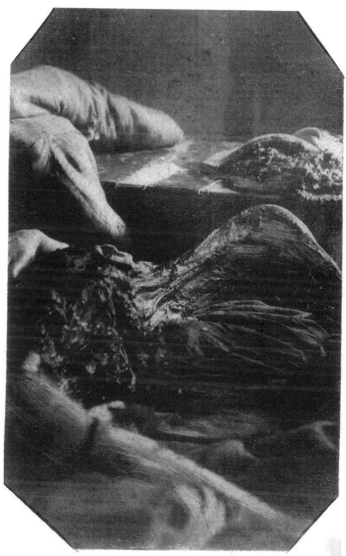

The second police photograph above is taken from the opposite direction towards the table and then the door / broken window(approximately from the foot of the bed). The mass on the table turned out to be a nose and thigh / leg flesh constructed in the form of a face.

These photographs (thanks to Wikipedia) are informative and show the true intensity of the rage and two examples of behaviour suggesting that the killer knew this victim. Stab marks were found through part of the blood stained bed sheet to the right of the head, indicating that it had been initially placed on the face during part of the attack. This, together with the facial representation / mock up on the table seems to suggest he could not look at the victims face while carrying out the mutilations.

This could also explain the mock up of the face afterwards. Not sick humour, as some have suggested but, in the murderers mind, sorry it had to be done as you did not take my advice, scorned me, made fun of me when I was drunk while singing your songs and thinking you were perhaps about to perhaps go back to a previous lover. Not to mention even go back on the game.

The poor unfortunate became very unfortunate in the final vicious, tragic (and maybe for Barnett) inevitable act.

A copy of Mary Kelly's death certificate.
Please note: "Otherwise Davies"

Martha Tabram

Was Martha Tabram (a London prostitute) the first victim?

The post-mortem examination was held by Dr. Timothy Kileen. The time of death was estimated as around 2.30–2.45 a.m. The focus of the wounds were the breasts, belly and groin areas. In his opinion all the wounds were inflicted by a right handed individual (Jack the Ripper was probably left handed). All but one wound seemed to have been inflicted by a penknife. There was one wound to the breast bone which seems to have been inflicted by a dagger or bayonet. This lead police to believe that a sailor was the perpetrator. All the killings were knife inflicted and involved impoverished prostitutes in the Whitechapel district. They were mostly carried out in darkness in the small hours of the morning, in a secluded site to which the public could gain access, and took place on or close to a weekend.

The day before Tabram's murder was the evening of a bank holiday. She is not always included among victim lists as her throat was not cut in the manner of later victims and she was not eviscerated. However serial killers usually increase the intensity and strengthen their M.O. as the series continues. Tabram's murder was, however, close to the geographical centre of the other killings.

Chapter 4

The Ripper Letters

More than 600 letters purporting to come from Jack The Ripper were sent to various newspapers at the time of the killing spree, however most were sent by thrill seekers, attention seekers and people who just wanted to get their writing into the press for cudos.

Here are details of the three, possibly genuine Jack the Ripper letters.

The Dear Boss letter dated 29th Sept 1888 sent to the Central News Agency was received three days before the Stride and Eddowes double murder.

It ran as follows (transcribed);

"Dear Boss,

I keep on hearing the police have caught me but they wont fix me just yet. I have laughed when they look so clever and talk about being on the right track. That joke about leather apron gave me real fits. I am down on whores and I shant quit ripping them till I do get buckled. Grand work the last job was. I gave the lady no time to squeal. How can they catch me now. I love my work and want to start again. You will soon hear of me with my funny little games. I saved some of the proper red stuff in a ginger beer bottle over the last job to write with but it went thick like glue and I cant use it. Red ink is fit enough I hope ha. Ha. The next job I do I shall clip the ladys ears off and send to the police officers just for jolly wouldn't you. Keep this letter back till I do a bit more work, then give it out straight. My knife's so nice and sharp I want to get to work right away if I get a chance. Good luck.

Yours truly

Jack the Ripper
Don't mind me giving the trade name

P.S. Wasnt good enough to post this before I got all the red ink off my hands curse it. No luck yet. They say I'm a doctor now. Ha Ha."

This Dear Boss letter seems to have been written as one would speak (this was suggested by police officer Paul Harrison in his book entitled Jack the Ripper the Mystery Solved).

The "Saucy Jacky" postcard.

This letter was received on the 1st of October 1888 at the Central News Agency.

I was not kidding dear old Boss when I gave you the tip, you'll hear about Saucy Jack's work tomorrow double event this time number one squealed a bit couldn't finish straight off. Ha, not the time to get ears for police. Thanks for keeping the letter back till I got to work again.

Jack the Ripper

And finally the From Hell letter which was sent to George Lusk (president of the Vigilance Committee) on the 16th of October 1888 in a three inch cubed box with what seemed like half a Human kidney preserved in spirits of wine (in the language of today it would have been preserved in ethanol).

Dr. Openshaw found it to be very similar to the kidney removed from the body of Catherine Eddowes. It also had evidence of Bright's disease (otherwise known as chronic inflammation of the kidney or nephritis—or glomerulonephritis).

"Mr. Lusk,
Sor

I send you half the Kidne I took from one woman and prasarved it for you tother piece I fried and ate it was very nise. I may send you the bloody knif that took it out if you wate a whil longer

Signed

Catch me when you can Mishter Lusk"

These are transcribed from the original scripts together with all the original spelling errors (assuming they are errors).

The From Hell letter is written at a much lower literacy level than the other two. One graphologist describes the style in the Ripper letters as indicating a cruel perverted sexuality. Another graphologist claims that the writing in the Lusk letter indicates it was written by Tumblety (her analysis is disputed). Even though forensic handwriting analysis is accepted by the courts as evidence and graphological analysis is not, it is still the best (a personal assessment) pseudoscience to provide clues to the identity of the Ripper. Knowing that many people may read the letters could have influenced the style by increasing the flamboyance, pressure and widths of flourishes. The suggestion that he might send the knife may indicate the end of the killing spree. This must be taken into account when trying to analyse the letters.

In a 1968 analysis of the From Hell letter, Canadian graphologist, C.M. MacLeod, writing in The Criminologist suggested this style exhibited tremendous drive in the vicious forward thrust of his overall writing, and great cunning in his covering-up of strokes. Also he would have had imagination as revealed in the upper-zone flourishes. Among other characteristics, the hooks on the t-bars indicated tenacity in achieving a goal. Over two hundred ripper letters were received by the police, newspapers and by the vigilance committee. However it is generally believed that the Dear Boss, Saucy Jack and From Hell communications are the only true ripper letters, the others being hoaxes from attention seekers. The Dear Boss letter went missing but was recovered in 1988. The use of sor for sir and prasarved for preserved indicates an Irish accent in the from hell letter. Emily Marsh who worked in a leather shop had a visit from a man with an Irish accent before the letter was posted, asking for the address of Mr. Lusk and the Vigilance Committee. Was this a coincidence, made up, or was he the killer or a friend of the killer?

Chapter 5

The Murder Sites Today

Martha Tabram—Gunthorpe street together with the arch that goes into it from Whitechapel High Street are still there but the block of flats off this street, where her body on a landing in George Yard buildings was found, has been demolished. The White Hart pub close by is where suspect George Chapman had a barber's shop in the basement.

Durward Street was the scene of the first murder. Within months of the killings local residence got the council to change the name from Bucks row to Durward Street. Modern flats in the old boarding school in the East end of Durward Street has a parking area to the left where the body of Mary Nichols was discovered.

The North side of Hanbury street survives to this day where in the back yard of no.29 Annie Chapman's body was found.

The yard off Berner street has been replaced by a modern school building—this was where Elizabeth Stride's body was found.

Mitre square is surrounded by modern office blocks now and a flower bed stands where the body of Catherine Eddowes was found.

Dorset Street, is still there, with modern industrial units.

Miller's court, where Mary Kelly was murdered at 4 a.m. (approximately), has been replaced by a food warehouse.

The Graves of the victims.

Mary Ann Nichols was buried in the City of London Cemetery at Manor Park. Elizabeth Stride was put to rest in the East London Cemetery.

Catherine Eddowes final resting place was the City of London Cemetery at Manor Park.

Mary Jane Kelly ended up in a grave at St. Patrick's Roman Catholic Cemetery in Leytonstone.

Annie Chapman had a common grave in the local Manor Park Cemetery, however its actual site has been lost due to multiple re-use over 127 years.

Chapter 6

The Whitechapel Vigilance Committees.

One of these Vigilance Committees was composed of businessmen, who were concerned that the murders were affecting trade in the area and therefore set up the best known group, The Whitechapel Vigilance Committee.

At the first meeting on the 10th September 1888 they elected a local builder George Lusk as their chairperson. As The Daily Telegraph reported on the 5th October 1888, the main members were:

"Drawn principally from the trading class, and include a builder, a cigar-manufacturer, a tailor, a picture-frame maker, a licensed victualler, and 'an actor'".

In September 1888 they wrote to the government to try to persuade them to offer a reward for information leading to the apprehension of the killer. When the Home Secretary Henry Matthews refused, the committee put up its own reward.

The committee also employed two private detectives, Mr. Le Grand and Mr. J.H. Batchelor, to investigate the murders in a separate capacity from the local police. The main link with the killer, however, surfaced on the 16th of October 1888 when the "From Hell" letter was received by the chairman George Lusk (to whom it was addressed) and it purported to have half of Eddowes's kidney inside preserved in alcohol. In the opinion of many Ripperologists this was the letter most likely to have been sent by the real killer. It would appear that he (the Ripper) took both the Police and the Vigilance Committee seriously as two organisations that could catch him and this provided two targets for his derision.

The committee were provided with whistles to aid in both communication and for sounding an alarm. This fact was well-known and could have boosted his confidence that if the Police communication methods (very similar) did not work then why should those of the Vigilance Committee?

There were other such committees. After Martha Tabram's murder 70 people elected 12 men to act as watchers calling themselves the St. Jude's Vigilance Committee (according to the Star of the 10th of September).

After the murder of Catherine Eddowes another Committee, The City Vigilance Committee was formed with Samuel Montagu as its chairman.

According to the Daily news of the 4th October 1888 another Committee formed by Labour delegates from East and Southeast London with Mr. L.H. Phillips as chairman was established.

Reynolds's newspaper reported on the 16th September 1888, that Jewish people also got together and formed the Jewish Vigilance Committee which intended to set up a reward for information leading to a successful arrest in the case.

Lastly the Spitalfields Vigilance Committee was formed and chaired by a Mr. Cohen. This committee wrote polite letters to various authorities suggesting that improved street lighting would help in catching the Ripper or at least providing fewer dark places for him to act out his vile deeds.

Mr. Lusk's committee, however, was the only one to receive, as far as we know, a letter from the Ripper himself.

Chapter 7

List of suspects

1. Francis Tumblety

He was named as the Ripper by authors Stewart Evans and Paul Gainey in the book The Lodger. This was after the discovery of the Littlechild letter in 1993 by Stewart Evans. In this letter dated 23rd September 1913 Littlechild states his suspicions about a certain doctor.

Born 1833 died 1903, Dr. Tumblety was in London round that time and was an Irish-American quack doctor (Indian type herbal doctor) and had a collection of wombs. He was arrested 7th Nov 1888 in London, for an act of gross indecency (of a homosexual nature), he also had a failed marriage to a woman he found out was a prostitute and he may have felt betrayed. His large moustache (which jutted out laterally and flamboyantly either side of his face) and because he was 6' 2"tall (and did not take Kelly's uterus) cut him out of the suspects list as far as I am concerned. However a modern psychic and onetime policeman stated he had strong vibes that this was the person after placing his hands on his photograph.

Detective Littlechild viewed him as a chief suspect. A leading graphologist has analysed his handwriting and it shows that he craved attention, has to have things his way and was a dominant character.

A lodger at 22 Batty Street, and an American doctor, returned there at 2a.m. fifteen minutes after the Eddowes murder and was found to have blood stained cuffs in his bag and immediately fled his lodgings. He was also known to be an abortionist in Canada.

But as for Jack the ripper Tumblety could not be him—see Marie Kelly murder—no obsessive, who collected uteri would ever leave one behind after carefully arranging all the organs, on a bedside table, between the feet and the uterus under the head and having the time, space and light to do it. Also being an abortionist he would not miss it—in case anyone argues on that point.

No way would he have had a key to her flat too. He also lied about his age. A recently found interview with Tumblety by the police, suggests two more interesting facts. One he was 6' 2" tall, taller than the general description of Jack the Ripper at the time, and two, he now had a downturned moustache and not the one portrayed in the media as sticking straight out either side more like the Jack the Ripper drawings in the newspapers after all. And his chin was clean shaven whereas all pictures published previously of Tumblety, showed a full beard too. He also stated he did not know that he had been followed by English detectives and knew of the Ripper crimes and was interested in the excitement and "queer scenes and sights".

It is also revealed that the homosexual incident was not the main reason he was arrested because the police had already linked the Whitechapel murders to him.

A coroner, Wynne Edwin Baxter stated that after one of the murders an American asked the curator of the Pathological museum for specimens from such killings and that he was willing to pay £20 each. The coroner thought that this could be a clue since if this person was willing to pay so much for these parts, what if he took it upon himself to get them for free?

In an article in the Pall Mall gazette dated 1st of October 1888 is stated that three pounds and five shillings would have bought a whole anatomical corpse. On the other hand this exonerates Tumblety, why would you pay for something you can get for free if you are the murderer? Assuming the rich American was Tumblety of course.

Oddly some state his height as 5' 10" and others between 5' 5" and 5' 7" in height. I extracted the 6' 2" height measurement from a police document which included his shoes. So I would place him between six foot and 5' 10 ".Dr. Fred Walker puts his height as 5' 11".

In spite of the odd height anomaly he is ruled out of any suspect final selection as he could not break his strong obsession with collecting uteri, and although one was excised it was not removed from the last victim's apartment, even though conditions were almost ideal.

Another point is that most descriptions of the Ripper put him at 30-35 years of age and Tumblety was much older. Some individuals who are fifty-five can look younger but twenty years younger, that would appear to stretch even an optimistic supporter of Tumblety being the Ripper.

However, as a fair minded person I must point out that similar murders took place abroad after the death of Mary Kelly and Tumblety was in those countries at the time. On the other hand, copycat killers did and do exist.

2. Walter Richard Sickert

This famous artist was born on the 31st of May 1860 and died on the 22nd of January 1942.

He painted prostitutes in similar poses as if dead and his former landlady told him this room was used by Jack the Ripper. He painted this room describing it as Jack the Ripper's bedroom.

Also he, with his artistic ability, could have produced forged Jack the Ripper letters to throw the police of the scent or the real letters, with disguised handwriting (being good at calligraphy). Little chance he is the one—why be fascinated by the story if you are the killer?

Mitochondrial analysis of the saliva under the stamp of a Sickert letter and that of the Ripper were supposed to be similar but with variation only in 12 genes and degradation who can say for sure. Handwritten letters from members of his family also show that Sickert was in France at the time of some of the murders. He was with his mother and brother in the late summer of that year (1888). He would not have been there for at least 4 of the murders.

The famous Victorian artist was named as the third man in the freemason conspiracy theory. Later his illegitimate son admitted he made the whole story up. However recently the case for him being considered as Jack The Ripper has been taken up by the American crime writer Patricia Cornwell who points out the prostitutes were posed as in his paintings in a similar way to how the bodies were found in the JTR killings and that stationery he used with water-marks have been shown to have been used in some of the ripper letters. I would point out anyone can see a pattern in postures and that unless the watermarked paper (theory repeated by the female author in November 2013 in newspaper articles) had been made by Sickert himself anyone can buy, borrow, find or steal paper.

3. Prince Albert Victor Christian Edward
(The Duke of Clarence)

A.k.a. Eddy-The grandson of Queen Victoria was born in 1864 and died in 1892.

He was supposed to have had casual sex with prostitutes in the Whitechapel area and this, it was claimed, resulted in a bastard child who had to be got rid of after a servant of Queen Victoria found out, but was he in France at the time of one of the murders?

There is a photograph of the prince shooting grouse at Balmoral 300 miles north of Whitechapel on a day when one of the murders took place.

Also if intestines placed over the left shoulder, indicates the craft or Freemasonry involvement, then why did two of the victims have their intestines placed over their right shoulders, if indeed a theory of freemason activity linked to Eddy is to be believed.

It has been suggested that solicitor Arthur Newton apparently conspired with the Government in hushing up Eddy's connections with Cleveland Street in 1889. The same solicitor is mentioned later in connection with Sickert and Robert Wood.

Wood, incidentally, acted as an artist's model for a series of paintings by Sickert.

Rumours abounded that Prince Eddie had secretly married a prostitute, Annie Crook, who was carrying his baby. To avoid a scandal Annie was supposedly locked away in an asylum. Mary Kelly, who had worked as a nursemaid to the prince and his wife may have attempted to blackmail the royal family, therefore Jack the Ripper (Gull and his associates in a carriage) was created to silence Kelly and the others she had told.

Not only did Sickert later claim the story was manufactured but the baby girl, said to have been the child of the Prince was born on April 18.1885, so she had to have been conceived at a time when Prince Eddy was in Germany, while Annie Crook, the alleged mother, was in London. Annie Crook did have a baby girl at that time called Alice and not from a dalliance with a prince. However this has not stopped a computer game and several books continuing this sensational but false story basically because it sounds so good.

4. Alfred Napier Blanchard

Who was a 34 year old canvasser, residing at 2 Rowland Grove, Hansworth, claimed in a drunken outburst in a pub to have committed the murders but was actually in Manchester at the time.

5. William Henry Bury

He was born on the 25th of May 1859 and died on the 24th April 1889, he married an ex-prostitute and kept a penknife under his pillow.

Inspector Abberline was sent north to see if this was the serial killer, as his method of stabbing his wife to death was in several ways similar to the murder of Poly Nichols (deep wound to the abdomen for example) also they were similar to penknife wounds on the body of Martha Tabram.

Someone had written on his door, using a stick of chalk, '*Jack the Ripper is in this sellar*'.

He had also left messages in his apartment stating 'Jack lives here'.

The evidence implicating this suspect seems to be tenuous at best. Bury walked into a Dundee police station and claimed that he must be Jack the Ripper after what he had just done to is wife. He was later tried, found guilty and hung on the 24th April 1889.

Inspector Abberline knew he lived in London at the time of the Whitechapel murders but did not believe it was anything more than a domestic incident gone wrong.

Bury claims he awoke after a night of drinking and found his wife on the floor with a rope around her neck. He panicked, stabbed the body with a knife (as you do.) and forced the body into a trunk breaking a leg in the process.

Earlier, before he and his former maid servant wife had moved to Dundee, he had forced her to part with shares she had inherited

(£20,000 worth) to allow him to set up as a sawdust dealer (together with horse and cart).

The obvious question is why was she working as a maid with all that money and why, with the means of support as well as a job would she ever consort with Bury?

6. Lewis Carroll

He was born on the 27th of January 1832 and died on the 14th of January 1898.

Revd. Charles Lutwidge Dodgson—author of children's books, (Alice's Adventures in Wonderland, Through the Looking-Glass & three other such books), mathematician, logician, Anglican deacon and photographer—wrote with purple ink in a secret diary except during days of the Whitechapel murders when he used black ink and had no alibi for each of those dates.

The average age of Ripper victims being 42 and his use of this number in mathematical games was another apparent coincidence. More like a mathematical pattern and fascination with no evil intent.

Suspected in the first place because of several obscure recondite anagrams in two of his stories.

Not considered of good enough health to have carried out the deeds too.

7. David Cohen

A.k.a. Nathan Kaminsky, Aaron Davis Cohen, (leather apron?) born 1865 died October 1889.

Insane Polish-Jew put in an asylum immediately after the last Ripper murder coincidence? See Aaron no.22 the Polish/Jew theory?

He was first suggested in Martin Fido's The Crimes, Detection and Death of Jack the Ripper (1987). Fido also states, in a recent article (Saturday, May 27ᵗʰ 2000), that Cohen was taken from an infirmary to an asylum under restraint. He did not state his name there and using local tradition where unnamed patients of Jewish extraction were called David Cohen instead of John Doe. This was untrue of Kosminsky. Along with Kosminski fit the psychological profile best.

He goes on to assert that the policeman Swanson somehow became confused on this point and thought they were one and the same person. Although this tailor has a different date of death from the other.

Died of exhaustion of mania—an expression possibly describing manic depressive bipolar condition. Described as having homicidal tendencies and a great hater of women.

What makes this a difficult section to research is that there were more than 1,500 Polish born tailors in London at the time. There may well be three separate individuals of similar origins here. However, a shawl belonging to Catherine Eddowes was sent for DNA analysis and showed (one DNA strand anyway) 100% match with present relatives of Kosminski in September 2014. However before we get over excited this only shows that a known Whitechapel resident knew a Whitechapel prostitute, highly likely in his case. It does not mean he murdered her—still it is interesting all the same.

8. Dr. Thomas Neill Cream

He was suggested as a possible Ripper suspect in the 1973 book The Gentleman from Chicago by author John Cashman.

Born in Glasgow on the 27th of May 1850 his family emigrated to Canada where he qualified in medicine at McGill University in 1876. He seduced a girl named Flora and after getting her pregnant performed a crude abortion leaving her in a much weakened state of health. He was forced to marry her (parental influence) but disappeared after the wedding and headed for England.

He worked for a while at St. Thomas's hospital in London in 1876 and it was thought he contracted syphilis from local prostitutes.

He returned to Canada and set up as an illegal abortionist in Ontario. He was reputed to have poisoned with chloroform a girl whom he was performing an abortion on but it was ruled she had committed suicide.

Then after a couple of cases of poisoning people with strychnine he was imprisoned for a life term at Joliet State Penitentiary in Illinois. He was released on 31st of July 1891 and came to England where he poisoned (over a period of months) four prostitutes with strychnine pills (Ellen Donworth, Matilda Clover, Emma Shivell and Alice Marsh.

Two prostitutes (including one who later died) described him as having glasses, bushy whiskers and being cross eyed.

He was arrested and found guilty and hung in Newgate prison on 15th November 1892. He was supposed to have said (just as the hangman was pulling the lever) 'I am Jack the ...'

He was in prison in the USA in 1888 for poisoning at the time of all the Ripper murders. At one point he wrote to the police claiming he knew who the Lambeth poisoner was and that he would like to claim the reward offered.

Why he was ever a suspect, apart from looking the part (and writing an incriminating letter to the police), is beyond me.

9. Frederick Bailey (Bayley) Deeming

(A.k.a.known as Mad Fred)

He employed several surname aliases during his life. These included Druin, Dawson, Duncan, Lawson and Williams.

He was born in 1842 and was executed in Australia for the murder of his four children and two wives in 1892.

He was a sailor who contracted a brain disease on a voyage and this altered his behaviour.

Another such influence on his behaviour was his unnaturally strong relationship with his mother and after her death in 1873 he became emotionally distraught for some time.

He married, had four children, became bankrupt, killed his wife and children in Merseyside, married again, killed his second wife and was arrested and was in jail in South Africa when the murders took place. Even so a Yesterday channel programme on the 7th March 2012 called prime suspect, believed it might be possible to match DNA found on artefacts at that time to him. He was also in jail in 1890 in Hull released in July 1891. A witness was found, who was a dressmaker, who knew Deeming as Lawson in 1888 around the time of the double murders. A shawl from one of the victims has been discovered framed and a larger part was bought at auction by a man living in Birkenhead. Deeming also carried an array of knives with him.

He claimed to be Jack the Ripper to fellow inmates and to a policeman. DNA was not found to match Deeming from either the shawl or from a stamp on one of the ripper letters. Under the stamp they found female DNA in the letter to Dr. Oppenshaw. Handwriting analysis of Deeming's will found few similarities to any Jack the ripper letters. However this is an interesting suspect.

He contracted syphilis from a prostitute and this made his life awful for two years. He swore to murder prostitutes after this event.

Was he the same Mr. Demming, a frequenter of the bar at the Singleton's Hotel in the Dargle in 1888 in South Africa? He did not pay his bills and organised a sumptuous tennis party catered for by the hotel.

An article in the New York Times dated the 29th of April 1892 stated that Deeming had confessed to his lawyers and the doctors who examined him that he had committed a majority of the "Jack the Ripper" crimes in the Whitechapel district of London.

Some newspapers circulated reports that he had not only been seen in the Whitechapel area at the time of the Ripper crimes but that he had also bought several knives.

He would have been 35 years old at the time of the Ripper murders and was described as fair haired with a large very obvious moustache, slight build and of medium height. His head was described as very small for a man of his stature.

After his conviction in Australia some press reports stated he had confessed to the last two Ripper murders.

Shortly after his execution a plaster death mask was sent to New Scotland Yard because of the rumours that he could have been Jack The Ripper.

For some time after it was on view in Scotland Yard's Black Museum and was described as that of Jack the Ripper.

10. Michael Ostrog

Born in 1833 and died circa 1904

Was a mad Russian doctor cruel to women and who carried surgical instruments.

He was described by the police as a homicidal maniac, habitually cruel to women who carried surgical knives in his pockets.

He was also a con man with many aliases: Claude Clayton, Dr. Grant, Count Sobieski, Dr. Barker and Bertrand Ashley, Max Grief Gossler, Max Kaife Gosslar, Grand Guidon, Stanislas Lublinski, Ashley Nabokoff, Orloff, Henry Ray, Max Sobieski plus a score of other names. He seems to have been nothing more than a demented conman.

On two occasions when police tried to arrest him he produced an eight-chambered revolver to effect a getaway. The first time he succeeded, the second time was in a Police station and the inspector grabbed the revolver and pointed it towards Ostrog who gave up. He conducted his own defence and got ten years in prison in 1874.

Released in 1883, later deported from France in 1886, he tried to steal a tankard, and later, in 1887 was tried under the name of Claude Clayton and pleaded insanity, but a Dr. Hillier stated that he thought that he was shamming and as a result he was handed down six months hard labour.

On the 30th September he was transferred to the Surrey Pauper Lunatic Asylum following a bout of mania (cause unknown). He was discharged, as a recovered individual on 10th March 1888.

He went to France where he was arrested by Parisian police for stealing a microscope on the 26th July 1888 (or according to the casebook of Jack the Ripper internet file August 1900 / was that not a 71 year old John Evest in London and not in Paris?).

He was sentenced on the 14th of November 1888 to two years in jail.

According to author Donald Rumbelow, Ostrog was in custody in France during the series of Whitechapel murders. With this in mind he cannot be considered a suspect any more.

11. Dr. Alexander Pedachenko—alias count Luskovo.

Born 1857. Died 1908.

Pedachenko was first offered as a suspect in 1928 by William Le Queux and later by Donald McCormick.

He was allegedly sent by the Russian secret police to discredit the London police. Later, if he even existed, he was thrown into a criminal lunatic asylum. This seems to be a story made up by one author and subsequently embellished by another.

It was also claimed in Dr. Dutton's Chronicles of Crime that he was the double of Severin Klosowski and that he worked as a barber-surgeon.

It was further claimed that he assisted a doctor in St. Saviour's Infirmary which was attended by four of the victims, Tabram, Chapman, Nichols and Kelly. In the Almanac de Gotha (1887 ed.) a major general Pedachenko is named but this may not be the same individual.

12. James Kenneth Stephen

This is a suspect put forward by Michael Harrison in 1972.

This suspect was born on the 25th of February 1859 and died on the 3rd of February 1892.

He was a physically strong, barrister and poet who was tutor to Prince Albert.

Apart from this, there does not seem to be any link to the murders. Again there is a suggested link to Gull and Freemasons (even though Gull was not a Mason). Suggestions have been made that he was one of several Masons tasked with tracking down the prostitutes and killing them one by one until they found the correct one, Annie Crook, with the child, Alice.

It was also claimed that a head injury (family rumours relate that he was struck by the vane of a windmill when his horse reared up and backed him into it, others say that he was hit by a projection from a moving train) in 1886 had left him mentally unstable (bipolar condition) and that he was possibly a homosexual lover of the Duke of Clarence, whom he tutored at Cambridge University during his stay there.

Apparently after he heard of the death of the Prince aged just 28 due to influenza he ate very little until his death 20 days later, aged 32.

His poetry was also quoted by Harrison in support of the suggestion that he hated women. However only one piece of supporting evidence can be found and that concerns a woman living in Newbury, who in 1975 claimed her great grandfather, a lawyer had stated to his daughter that he knew the police suspected Stephen of being the Ripper.

13. Francis Thompson

Born on the 18th of December 1859 and died on the 13th of November 1907.

Was a poet and opium addict, after having being prescribed laudanum for a serious lung infection in 1879.

A sometime vagrant in London, he was put up by a prostitute and sold poetry.

The only link to him being a suspect was that he was in London at the time.

However there is the theory that each murder was on a feast day of a martyr and these corresponded to the patron saints of innocence, butchers, soldiers, doctors and scholars as well as being the 5 crucifixion wounds of Christ using these stigmata for immediate social effect and saving the killer from damnation in the process. Thompson was a deeply religious man.

He may well have been too high on drugs to have been able to produce any kind of serial murder pattern and not get caught.

The reasons for some having suspected him of being the Ripper were probably that he frequented the East End of London as an addict vagrant, consorted with prostitutes, carried a knife and owned a leather apron. He also wrote poetry with themes incorporating medieval men who mutilated women.

14. Dr. John Williams

Born on the 6th of November 1840 and died on the 24th of May 1926 and was obsessed by the fact that his wife could not conceive and bear him a child and he became obsessed with female anatomy and infertility.

He also worked at the Whitechapel workhouse where he treated Mary Ann Nichols and three other Ripper victims.

His great grand-nephew suspected he was the Ripper.

He was the obstetrician to Queen Victoria's daughter and was supposed to have killed and mutilated, with a blunted knife, in an attempt to research the causes of infertility. Possibly the last person in the world who would employ a blunted knife as he was not only well off, had access to excellent surgical equipment but would only use surgical instruments(always kept clean and sharp) for any such dissections—assuming the theory has any basis.

Suspect was proposed by Tony Williams (his nephew) and Humphrey Price in 2005. In the book Uncle Jack it was suggested that a six inch scalpel with a broken point was found among is effects and a further suggestion was connected with diary entries which placed him in Whitechapel around the time of Annie Chapman's murder and that he treated Poly Nichols. However there is controversy surrounding whether or not the diary had been altered.

Another point is that Dr. Williams wrote to Dr. Morgan Davies (see D'Onston Stephenson section) who was another Jack the Ripper suspect. He states in the letter that he is sorry they could not meet as he would now be attending a clinic in Whitechapel. The letter was dated 8th September 1888 the date the second Ripper victim was murdered in Hanbury Street.

15. Montague John Druitt

Born on August the 15th 1857 was a barrister who could not get a full brief and so lack of money forced him into teaching. He became assistant schoolmaster (or usher) in a private all boys school but was dismissed in November 1888, reason not given, although Mr. Valentine, who dismissed him, indicated that it was of a serious nature. It was reported by the Southern Guardian on 1st Jan 1889 that he had left the headmaster a letter suggesting suicidal thoughts, and later was found in the river Thames off Thorneycroft's torpedo works near Chiswick with stones in his pockets, some money, a train ticket and his last pay cheque (including severance pay) on December 31st 1888.

According to the Dorset Chronicle in an article dated Thursday 10th January 1889, a £50 cheque and £16 in gold were found with the body.

However according to author Donald Rumbelow he had £2 10s in gold, some change, and two cheques drawn on the London and Provincial Bank. One for £50 and the other for £16.

Suspected by the police (especially Melville Macnaghten at the time), he was described as sexually insane, a Victorian phrase meaning homosexual.

It appears he drowned himself because his mother went mad and he thought the same was happening to him. His suicide note suggested as much. In fact it stated:-

'Since Friday I felt I was going to be like Mother and the best thing for me was to die'.

Faked papers too implicated him.

He also had a lifelong friendship with his cousin Emily who finally went to the police about him.

Several sources have suggested that his family suspected that he was Jack the Ripper.

Handwriting analysis, by a leading graphologist, shows variation in pressure indicating a worrier.

To play cricket between murders in spotless clothes, and his personality which was more gentle and withdrawn than aggressive and dominant indicate to me that he could not have been the elusive killer.

Also It would have been difficult to have murdered Annie Chapman at 5.30a.m., washed up and boarded the train for Blackheath in time for an 11.30 a.m. cricket match(where he presented him self without a single blood stain).

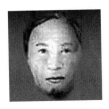

16. Carl Feigenbaum
(Anton Zahn, Carl Strobohn, Karl Zahn)

A murderer who was a sailor and was in London at the time and possessed lots of aliases. I mention just three, but even his original name may not have the correct spelling.

He was arrested in 1894 and executed in 1896.

It was when he was in lodgings with Mrs. Hobson and her son he tried to steal a sum of money and was interrupted and slit the throat of the woman with the knife he was using, as one suggestion goes, to prize open a cash box in order to take part of the money. She managed to shout murder out of the window. He ran down the street and was arrested, after first trying to put the police off by claiming it was not him.

His lawyer stated that he hated and was violent towards women and that he believed (he stated all this after his former client was hung for murder) that he was Jack the Ripper in a press conference outside Sing Sing prison where his lawyer actually claimed he had done research showing Carl had been in Whitechapel at the time of the murders.

However the partner of the lawyer, at the time disagreed with the latter assertion.

Some link him with a total of nine murders including two in America. Although he never confessed to being Jack the Ripper and with one of his victims he had theft as a motive, he was ingenious, pretending to be stupid when he certainly was not, and was sadistic towards women.

This is a character suspected by author Trevor Marriott.

However this presupposes there were no willing prostitutes who hung round the docks—why look further afield?

Also has he lost the slashing and removing of internal organs MO which he had, if he was Jack the Ripper, so completely built up by now?

Is it only the similarity of the murders in America and London which keep this suspect in the light?

If it could be shown employing ship manifests that Carl had been in London on all the dates when victims died then it would be a different story.

17. Fogelma

A single named epithet for a suspect who died in 1902.

This individual was a Norwegian sailor who ended up in a lunatic asylum in Morris Plains, New Jersey, in 1899. He had been heard muttering scenes and incidents connecting him with 1888 London Ripper crimes. Bogus story?. Possibly from one newspaper article?

According to the Complete Jack the Ripper A to Z research has shown that Morris Plains Asylum (now called the Greystone Park Psychiatric Hospital) has no record of a past patient named Fogelma.

18. Br. George Hutchinson

Did he describe the man outside Kelly's room just too well? Why was he lurking there for such a long time? Was he just a peeping Tom?

He was an unemployed groom / labourer / night watchman and some say his description of the Ripper was so good that it was the Ripper trying to confuse the issue.

His description goes roughly like this;

He was a well-dressed man approximately 5' 6" in height 34 or 35 years old, with a dark complexion and a dark moustache which was turned up at the ends, (Tumblety had his straight pointed out at the sides and Joe Barnett had his turned down), a horseshoe tie pin on his dark necktie, dark spats and a waistcoat with a large gold chain. His watch chain had a big seal with a red stone hanging from it. His chin was clean shaven. He carried a small parcel, about eight inches long in his hand with a strap round it (wrapped in a type of American style cloth). He had brown kid gloves in his free hand and wore a long Astrakhan coat. He also had dark eyes (Joe Barnett had blue eyes) and walked very softly.

Since he supplied that kind of detail, was he wondering if he could mug this apparently rich gentleman or was it a total fabrication to divert attention from himself or was there another explanation?

No wonder he has been considered a strong suspect himself.

He lived in the Victoria Home for Working Men 39-41 Commercial Street. He was 22/23 years old, the correct build for the Ripper and was short and stout. Some have suggested that his description of the man with Mary Kelly early that morning as having sandy eyelashes is just too much by way of intricate detail suggesting that it was just a fabrication.

In any case I cannot find a date of birth or death for this individual, so he must just, unsatisfactorily, remain in the shadows for the moment.

He was paid a sum of money by the police for his help and was given a sum of money by a newspaper for his story. Was that his motivation?

It is also interesting that Hutchinson, who probably knew Joe Barnett by sight, did not claim to have seen him with Mary Kelly then, unless he assumed that Joe was always around and that the police would understand that and therefore he would not have to mention any sightings of Barnett.

19. Hyam Hyams

He was born in Aldgate on the 8th February 1855 and was a simple fruit seller, an alcoholic, mentally unstable and a wife beater. His father made cigars near to the crimes. He was once reputed to have slashed an orderly across the neck in an asylum.

Pictures of him show a confused simple man—hardly a serial killer with a plan.

He died in Colney Hatch Lunatic Asylum on the 22nd of March 1913.

However at the time one could see how he became a suspect due to his violence, attacking people with knives and being placed in an asylum some seven weeks after the Mary Kelly murder after which the Ripper series of murders seemed to stop.

20. James Kelly

A paranoid schizophrenic who murdered his wife and blamed Whitechapel prostitutes for giving him Venereal disease.

Born April 20th 1860 died 1929.

He left school in 1873 and took an apprenticeship as an upholsterer.

In 1875 he hears he is to inherit £25,000 when he reaches 25.

He went to a commercial academy in New Brighton to acquire bookkeeping and clerical skills.

In 1877 he obtained a position with a Liverpool pawnbroker. He started at this point to act irrationally and get mood swings.

In 1878 he moved to London. A period of hard drinking, paid sex and work in sweatshops followed.

In 1882 he finds that he cannot penetrate his girlfriend, Sara, yet had no difficulty with prostitutes.

In 1883 after marrying Sara and killing her, he is charged, goes for trial, is found guilty, but commuted sentence to life in a secure criminal asylum.

January 23rd 1888 he escaped from the asylum. A poor record of his time in London exists until he presents himself, years later at Broadmoor on 11th Feb 1927 and remained there for the rest of his life.

However as he was around in London during the period covering all the Ripper killings he is a suspect.

21. Severin Antoniovich Klosowski (George Chapman)

Polish serial killer and son of a carpenter, he was apprenticed to a surgeon and was a barber's assistant in London at the time of the murders.

Born on 14th Dec 1865 and died by execution on 7th April 1903 after poisoning three women.

Over the years he took several mistresses who posed as his wives. Motives for killing three of them were not clear but the first 'wife' would have netted him £500 after her death.

He was a violent man with a misogynistic streak and known to have beaten his 'wives'.

He however was inspector Abberline's suspect after his arrest for wife murder in 1903.

According to the Fort Wayne News, Indiana, U.S.A. in an article dated 23rd March 1903 (referring to his conviction in a trial the previous Thursday) he left Whitechapel after the Ripper murders and went to Jersey City where he opened a barber's shop and it was there that he murdered several women. His real wife (according to the same article) informed the police that he tried to kill her also in a bedroom at the rear of the barber's shop.

It was also alleged in 1930 by Hargrave L. Adam that he had been suspected around the time of the murders.

22. Aaron Mordke Kosminski

Born 1865 and died 1919.

Identified and expanded from the surname by Martin Fido and thus fully identifying him from the Kosminski mentioned in the Macnaghten memoranda and the suspect of Robert Anderson in the Swanson marginalia.

This suspect was a Polish Jew admitted to a lunatic asylum 1891.

He is probably the same person as David Cohen, although the date of death is recorded as two different dates.

He was thought of as the chief suspect, at the time, by two of the highest ranked police officers.

Many years later, two retired City of London officers, Sagar and Cox talked of observing the odd behaviour of a Polish-Jew butcher in Butchers Row, and, noticing that he was being observed, he stayed on the premises, not perhaps wishing the officers to find out where he lived.

Their profile suggests: a Jew and working either as a butcher / butcher's assistant or a meat salesman. That he probably lived in the East End of London and that his motive was probably revenge against prostitutes. Along with Kosminski fit the psychological profile best.

A witness refused to give evidence against him as he was a fellow Jew and he assumed that his evidence could hang him. In Naming Jack the Ripper an interesting book published in 2014(by Russell Edwards) it was claimed that semen stains proved to be on Catherine Eddowes shawl using mitochondrial DNA analysis proved that he was the killer. This does not preclude the fact that he lived in the area and as a mentally ill person could have ejaculated over her in a primitive sexual response et cetera. According to modern e-profile and psychological analysis (e.g. by Laura Richards) these murders were not the work of a mad man. So interesting new / style research but it only shows a physical connection of this suspect to one of the victims and not that he attacked her.

23. Jacob Hyam Levy

Born 1856 and died 1891. He was a butcher who ultimately went mad and lived close to the murdered women.

He was a Jew who sponsored Martin Kosminski (not connected to Aaron Kosminski) in his 1877 naturalisation application.

Levy was a London born Spitalfields butcher who was one of three witnesses on the night of Catherine Eddowes murder.

He is a suspect recently suggested by Mark King in Ripperologist publication (1999 & 2000). He suggested that he knew Joseph Hyam Levy and that Joseph recognised him as the man with Catherine Eddowes outside Church passage. He went on to speculate that Levy's syphilis was his motivation to kill prostitutes and that he dropped the piece of Catherine Eddowes' apron in Goulston Street to put the police off the assertion that he was heading further east from Middlesex Street.

No evidence has been found to substantiate any of these claims.

24. James Maybrick

Born 25th Oct 1838 and died 11th May 1889. Had many mistresses and his wife also had an affair.

He was a Liverpool cotton merchant poisoned to death by his wife, an American woman, who in her trial was treated in a biased manner by the man who presided over the court case.

He was also the father of another suspect J.K. Stephen who was apparently losing his mind, as some evidence that James Maybrick used arsenic poison as an aphrodisiac was not presented at trial and the claims that he was the Ripper were probably just hoaxes.

The main one of which was: In 1993 a diary was found in which Maybrick confessed to being Jack the Ripper. However the ink used to write the diary was not only scripted in a different handwriting style to the suspect but had, as part of its composition, a preservative not marketed until 1974 (a chemical called chloroacetamide). However, later research suggests this chemical was known in 1889.

One could also postulate that even if the diary (and later a watch inscribed with the victim's names) turned out to be hoaxes he could have had an obsession with the character of Jack the Ripper who might, in his eyes at least, have been the man he could never be.

It is easy to see how you could hoax a Ripper diary. First buy an old (circa 1888) scrap book. Then use a razor blade to scrape off the ink or use special dry cleaning solvent to remove it or non-ink writing and employ a similar style to the Dear Boss letter using red ink. Unfortunately, as we have just seen, the ink will be your undoing. Because unless you purchase a Victorian ink well, with dried ink in it and dissolve the old ink in alcohol, the chemical composition of the mixture of dyes and preservatives that constitutes modern ink will find you out. So I have eliminated this suspect from contenders for the Jack the Ripper role.

25. Alois Szemeredy

Born in 1840 and died 1892

He was both a soldier and a butcher. He posed in London as Argentinean businessman Alonzo Maduro at that time.

Born in Pest one of the two cities either side of the Danube, later to become Budapest on 7th July 1840.

He enlisted at an early age in the Austro-Hungarian army. He received a certificate for good conduct and listed as a tanner. He later received another certificate for good conduct, this time he was listed as a butcher.

He then deserted on the 29th June 1863.

In October 1865 he presented himself at the Argentinean consulate in Genoa, and on March 17th 1866 he joined the Argentinean army.

In May he was declared insane. He was placed in an asylum from where he escaped on the 17th September.

He took up a new occupation as a barber and then stole a large sum of money and in 1873 was charged with attempted murder. He escaped and became a self-styled doctor practising medicine in 1889 in Junin.

Afterwards he moved to Uruguay where he was accused of the murder of Carolina Metz.

He slit his throat with a razor blade in 1892, was this just to make a gruesome point or was it a genuine suicide attempt?

In 1888 he came to London posing as an Argentinean businessman, Alonzo Maduro.

Because of the way he apparently slit the throat of Carolina Metz with a long thin sheaf knife people have linked him with the Ripper murders.

He was well-travelled, had a bad temper, was a thief and a con man, could use a knife and had a little medical knowledge. But no vendetta against prostitutes in Whitechapel can be ascribed to this well-travelled villain.

26. Robert D'Onston Stephenson

Born 1841. Died 1916.

Robert, aka Roslyn, was a writer and follower of the black arts who had theories on Jack the ripper. His occult name was Tautridelta, which he used as a pen-name too. It means triple triangle of Pythagoras—a strong magical symbol.

In my opinion, not a serious contender.

He was a doctor of medicine with qualifications from Paris and New York. He reported to the police at the time, but was so erudite and helpful he was dismissed as harmless.

In a newspaper article it was suggested that the murders formed the pattern of a profane cross.

In 1940's, A. Crowley, a chess player, climber, poet and occultist said he had bought a box with five white bloody ties in it purporting to have been the property of Jack the Ripper. He claimed he had bought it from Dr. Roslyn D'Onston who shared an interest in 'esoteric' artifacts. This tie box actually belonged to Vittoria Cremers a friend of Roslyn D'Onston Stephenson.

This was a load of rubbish for another reason. Vittoria Cremers became the business manager of A. Crowley in 1914, so he understood perfectly well that the ties were not from Jack the ripper.

Another source states that Vittoria saw a box with books and black ties with dull brown stains in the possession of Roslyn.

A further story in Crowley's book Confessions states that Cremers picked the lock of a box held by cords under Stephenson's bed and found white dress ties black with clotted blood.

Whose story you believe on the box saga is up to you.

Crowley, therefore, claims it was one of her stories in his autobiography.

A further twist to the ties saga concerns Betty May, a model, who claimed that Crowley owned the Jack the Ripper neck ties. Since she claimed this around 1925 it must be assumed that she was only repeating Cremer's version but with a twist added to get back at Crowley because her ex-husband Raoul Loveday died at the Abbey of Thelema, in Sicily (from enteritis) where Crowley had his " do what thou wilt" phase.

Roslyn also wrote a letter claiming a reward of £1000 for information leading to the arrest of the Ripper (even though only £500 was being offered at the time) with details of a Dr. Morgan Davies he knew from hospital when he was treated for typhoid infection and who suggested vile sexual approaches towards women.

Roslyn was interviewed by the police who did not believe action was necessary. His cross theory, which has 7 of the murders forming the pattern of the Calvary cross was looked at by a professor of statistics and he claimed that the odds against D'Onston's Ripper Cross scenario being wrong were one in 15,249,024.

It has also been suggested that one of the bodies was probably moved, out of the line of sight, or to improve the pattern.

27. Sir William Withey Gull

Born 1816 died 1890.

Robert James Lees was a medium who supposedly tracked Gull down as the serial killer Jack the Ripper. He related the story that he found Dr. Gull insane, masquerading as a patient called Thomas Mason. There was talk of a fake funeral as well, and the grave being too large for him and his wife alone.

However this eminent doctor was too ill and not of a violent temperament to have had a hand—unless associated with Freemason type help—in the Jack the Ripper murders.

He was stated that he was a mason and had the ear of Queen Victoria but at the time of the murders he was 72 and had already had one heart attack and a stroke which left him much weakened.

More recent research suggests he was not a freemason after all.

It would appear that he would not have had either the inclination or the physical stamina to have carried out these murders, (with or without help), and would have stood out like a sore thumb especially at 8.30 a.m. on the day of the last murder.

28. Thomas Hayne Cutbush

He was a psychotic individual, born in 1866, who stabbed a woman with a dagger.

The knife he used was different in shape from that which the Ripper appeared to use and was purchased in February 1891, two years and three months after the last Ripper murder.

Cutbush also had an uncle who was a police officer and a police memo suggesting three different suspects was perhaps written to turn attention away from him as a suspect.

Cutbush had a disturbed and violent youth. He became insane in 1888, the year of the killings, and was wandering the streets of London. He was sent to Lambeth infirmary in 1891 suffering delusions thought to have been caused by syphilis. However he immediately escaped and stabbed a woman and attempted to stab another. He was again detained, pronounced insane and sent to Broadmoor in 1891 where he stayed until his death in 1903. On 30.09.13 a British TV documentary on Dartmoor secure mental hospital looked at old files on Cutbush and an author suggested, again, that he was Jack The Ripper. I have 7 problems with this assertion: 1. He was too tall 5' 9" JTR was 5' 6" max. 2. He sported a thin moustache and not a thick one that JTR had. 3. His moustache was black and not carroty. 4. He was 26 and not approx. 35 as JTR profiles indicate. 5. He was of thin build and JTR was medium to stocky build. My sixth point (backed up by modern Scotland Yard profiling) is that he was sane and normal, Cutbush was mentally ill. Finally Cutbush stabbed women in the buttocks, bad yes, but nowhere near the level of sadistic brutality demonstrated by JTR in his criminal spree. Leather apron and Ripperologist on Twitter agree with me on this last point.

29. Joseph Silver

Born 1868 died 1917

Polish born Joseph Silver arrived in Johannesburg in 1898 from Sing Sing where he was detained for burglary and a stay in London 10 years earlier.

He wrote several bold letters to newspapers and used many aliases.

He was a pimp and brothel keeper and would have been familiar with prostitutes in the Whitechapel area.

He was tracked by the son of a detective several years later across Africa, The Americas and Europe, therefore he was very widely travelled.

He had a history of hating women and had a record of being violent towards them.

He was also one of a number of Polish Jews who were connected with the murders.

A South African historian, Charles van Onselen stated that Silver was in Whitechapel at the time of the murders as there is evidence his daughter was born there. See Joseph Lis no.169.

30. Robert Mann

Circa 1830–92

This individual was a mortuary attendant from Whitechapel who came from a broken home. He had sufficient medical knowledge and had undressed the victim Polly Nichols (with the help of an assistant) when told not to by Inspector Spratling. Was this possibly to admire his own technique or was he a pervert or just curious? This is fair as far as FBI psychological profiles go but it appears to be too coincidental and obvious.

He was described by coroner Wynne Baxter as being unreliable and suffering from fits. However medical knowledge and curiosity, together with the psychological profile do not, in my opinion, constitute condign evidence of his guilt. This however is a new theory and suspect (put forward by historian Mei Trow in 2009) and no doubt more links between him and the killer will be unearthed in due course. Eddowes kidney (the part of which was pickled and sent to Mr. Lusk) had its renal artery trimmed (according to Dr. Brown) so could not be matched to the victim. Also Medical students at the time sometimes sent pickled organs through the post as a joke. Finally anyone could have bought neat alcohol / Vodka and pickled it not just a medical person or the mortuary attendant. Plus he was 58 at the time of the murders and suffering from epilepsy and tuberculosis and how could he have had the key to Mary Kelly's room?

31. Dick Austin

Austin was a sailor, later soldier, hater of women and stated that he would "kill every whore and cut her inside out".

He was known to be in the habit of grinding his teeth in anger.

James Oliver, another soldier who knew him, had named him as the Ripper.

Abberline ordered that all divisions should be contacted for information. No result was forthcoming.

The Dear Boss letter was shown to Oliver who said it much resembled Austin's handwriting.

Only one Richard Austin is in 1881 census registered at cavalry barracks, Barrack Street, Pockthorpe, Norfolk in the private 3rd Hussars, aged 32, born 1849 in Bexley Kent and unmarried.

32. Charles R.(P.)Hammond

This person was a well known brothel proprietor. He was connected with the Cleveland Street scandal in 1889 and was convicted of larceny.

Although he may have known all the victims, little other evidence of his link to the Ripper murders can be found.

However the original story surfaced when P.C. 718, Luke Hants of the General Post Office's own police force, stopped and interrogated a 15 year old telegraph boy called Charles Swinscow, who worked at St. Martin's Le Grand and who had been found carrying 18 shillings. This approximated to a couple of months wages. He was immediately accused of stealing. Swinscow protested that he had earned the money by "going to bed with gentlemen" at the rate of four shillings a time at Number 19 Cleveland Street. Hammond had kept the other sixteen shillings of each sovereign that customers paid for the boy's services.

Various Lords, Earls and one Colonel were reputed to frequent the brothel (some also say so did Prince Eddy) and the affair was to cause the Prime Minister Lord Salisbury a good deal of embarrassment. Meanwhile Hammond escaped to France—immoral, a pimp, but no serial killer.

33. Dr. Morgan Davies

Born in 1854 and died in 1920.

Davies described sodomy of one Jack the Ripper victims, (Mary Kelly) and suggested behavioural patterns for the Ripper.

The way he acted out the scenes made others suspicious of his motive/involvement. This could have just been histrionics to entertain and/or impress the patients while he was visiting a sick friend, Dr. Evans, or to entertain his friend who was in the same ward as D'Onston Stephenson.

D'Onston was said to have witnessed this display whilst recovering from typhus. Or it could have been an embellished account by D'Onston Stephenson on the 26th December 1888 i.e. either attention seeking by D'Onston Stephenson or an interesting possible suspect brought to the attention of the police by the same in return for a monetary reward which he would have used for drugs, drink or both.

34. John Pizer

Circa.1850–1897

Detective Thick (e) arrested Pizer but later released without charge.

Pizer claimed since the officer had known him for years that it was based on animosity rather than evidence.

He was one of a number of suspects known as "leather apron" and was a boot maker from the Whitechapel area who was arrested for minor assaults on prostitutes.

A Star newspaper reporter stated that at least 50 women had described a man who had been ill treating them. They described him as being 5' 4" in height and wearing a dark close fitting cap, being thickset with black hair and a small black moustache and being aged between 38 and 40, but as it turns out, he had alibis for two of the murders (staying with relatives and watching a large fire at London docklands) and was released.

"Gabriel Pizer is prepared to prove that John Pizer came to his house on Thursday last, and that he remained indoors until Monday".

This is a quote from an edition of the Daily Telegraph on Wednesday, September 12th 1888. The article also stated that he was placed in a twenty men line up and was recognised as being in the area around the time of the Eddowes murder and that on being picked out in the line up he exclaimed "what, you know me?"

Also, leather apron was an epithet referred to in the Dear Boss letter, supposedly from Jack the ripper himself—where he appears to have a laugh at the expense of the police suggesting that they were on the wrong track.

35. James Thomas Sadler

Born 1838, Sadler was a man who worked as a hackney carriage driver until 1878 and then as an omnibus conductor.

He was addicted to drink and consorted with prostitutes. He was a suspect but proved he was at sea at the time of the earlier murders. He was arrested and released.

In 1891 after the murder of Frances Coles, whom he was seen talking to earlier and with whom he spent the night then later drank with her in several pubs until he was mugged and because she did not assist or call for help, they parted company. He was arrested again, and again released without charge.

36. H.P. Blavatsky

He was theosophist and occultist whom Alister Crowley, in an essay in 1913, claimed was a female Jack the ripper. No evidence has been found so far for this claim.

37. Thomas Vere Bayne

Vere Bayne was born in 1829 and died in 1908.

Through obscure anagrams in the writings of two of Lewis Carroll's works it was surmised that this colleague of Carroll helped him commit these murders.

However both had alibis for some of the murders and both were in a poor state of health at the time.

The theory linking him and lifelong friend Carroll in the Jack the Ripper spree was a theory of the writer Richard Wallace (1996).

38. Randolph Spencer Churchill

Born 1849. Died 1894.

This suspect was first alleged in 1991.

He was supposedly linked together with other freemasons, being the highest freemason in England at the time, in a murder plot associated with Mary Kelly and other prostitutes to cover up Eddie's bastard child episode. This link appears Tenuous to say the least.

39. Dr. Merchant

Born 1851. Died 1888.

In 1931 a retired metropolitan police constable Robert Spicer gave his story to the Express newspaper. He was on patrol and came across a well-dressed man with blood spots on his shirt cuffs and carrying a Gladstone bag and sitting with a known prostitute called Rosie. This was a short time after the murder of two prostitutes. He asked what he was doing and he replied that it was none of his business. The officer arrested him and the prostitute and back at the station the doctor handed them his professional card. The Gladstone bag was never searched and he stated he was doing social work among the community of prostitutes. He was released and the constable was told off for such a petty arrest. What was in the bag? Let us assume it was general medical equipment and medicines and not a ripper knife and/or chloroform.

It is also claimed that he was a pseudonym invented by B.E. Riley to hide the identity of an alleged suspect.

His death shortly after the murders could be regarded as a coincidence.

40. Robert Wood

This Camden town murder suspect, who, along with Walter Sickert has been linked to the Ripper killings.

He designed glassware for the sand and blast manufacturing company in Gray's Inn road in 1907.

He was tried for the murder of a young prostitute Phyllis Dimmock (real name Emily) whom he sent a postcard to meet him in a pub. Jack the Ripper was known to have sent one postcard.

He was allowed to appear in the witness box himself, the first time in British legal history. Newton his solicitor was an associate of Walter Sickert and also linked to the Ripper murders. He claimed that it was two years later when he first met Emily, and he stuck to this story.

Crabtree, who was in prison at the time, fingered Wood with one of his descriptions as a young person with artistic hands who was a friend of Emily in 1905.In the courthouse the jury considered the evidence in only a quarter of an hour and pronounced him "not guilty". Some observers thought Wood was an excellent liar, however the verdict stood. The crime in Camden was not as grisly as the ones 19 years earlier, did the murderer change his signature or is there no link?

41. G. Wentworth Bell-Smith

A Canadian lodger in London at that time from Toronto, Smith had loaded firearms in his lodgings. This was brought to the attention of the local police who found that his possession of them was legitimate, but also recorded that he was a religious zealot with a deep hatred for prostitutes.

However they did not feel he was a danger to women of the streets or to the general public.

Someone suggested, after he arrived back at 4.00 a.m. with red stains on his boots, that this was odd. However the so-called stains turned out to be no more than red mud.

Also, no mention of any G. Wentworth Bell-Smith of the correct age can be found in Ontario archives. The only entry for a Henry Wentworth Bell-Smith shows that he would have been too young at the time.

42. Mr. Charles Cross (Crass)

This was the name that this suspect gave to everyone at the time, although his father's name was Lechmere.

He was born in 1849 and died in 1920.

He lived at 22 Doveton Street, Bethnal Green.

He was a cart driver for Pickfords who had been seen standing over the body of Polly Nichols, the first victim, in Bucks row and was the only person to have been recorded near the corpse of a victim. At the inquest, Robert Paul stated that as he approached the area he saw a man standing in the middle of the road. He stated that he hung around because he feared that the murderer was close at hand.

Every day he would have walked back and forth through the killing area. Is he a suspect or just a witness?

It is also odd to note that he did not give his true surname to the police, yet he used it throughout his life up to the point of the Ripper murders.

And not just his surname could have been altered, as PC Jonas Mizen (55H) referred to him as a Mr. George Cross.

Or, since PC Mizen's assertion was quoted in the Morning Advertiser dated the 4th September 1888, they could have confused the name (but not with the medal which was not introduced until 24th September 1940).

On Channel 5 T.V. on the 17th of November 2014, in a programme called 'Jack the Ripper. The missing evidence' by Christer Holgrem, a journalist, it was stated that as a cart driver (carman) his route took him by all the murder scenes between 2 and 3 am. However, Mary Jane Kelly was murdered later in the hours of daylight and no cart was seen anywhere near at the time. Another interesting theory but little to back it up.

43. Robert Paul

Paul was also a carter also with Pickfords. He was called over by Charles Cross to what looked like a tarpaulin when on his way to work at 3.45 a.m. Charles thought it might be useful in his line of work. However, it turned out to be the bundle of clothes Poly Nichols was wearing.

Was he somehow connected or just a casual passerby?

44. Jacob Isenschmid

Born on the 20th April 1843 in Buch, Switzerland, he was known as the Mad Pork Butcher. He was known to have stayed out late at night and was absent from his lodgings after Annie Chapman's murder.

His wife Mary stated that he was often in the habit of carrying large knives around with him.

Some locals remember him sharpening knives in the street and calling himself Leather Apron.

He was arrested on 12th Sept 1888 and was taken to Holloway police station where he was adjudged to be insane and was sent to an asylum.

A reporter for the halfpenny London newspaper The Star for an article dated 18th September 1888 stated that the butcher had had sunstroke and year on year after that went through a mad phase.

He could not have understood that above 42 degrees Celsius the body proteins (especially enzymes which control and catalyse body metabolism) become denatured or cooked. Also they did not understand that an imbalance in the biochemical processes in the brain and a genetic predisposition to abnormal psychological processes coupled with a crisis can precipitate a mental illness.

Such a crisis was precipitated in Jacob when in 1887 his business failed and he was confined to Colney Hatch Asylum according to The Complete Jack The Ripper A-Z by Paul Begg, Martin Fido and Keith Skinner (published in hardback 2010). This excellent reference guide also states that he could not have been Jack The Ripper because he was incarcerated during the period covering the later murders.

I suspect that he was too loud and obvious a character, drawing considerable attention to himself. In contrast, The Rippers MO is more than just the work of a madman.

45. Charles Ludwig. Also called Weitzel or Wetzel

Ludwig was a German hairdresser born in 1848.

He was dismissed from one establishment for dirty habits. He had threatened a man with a long thin knife because he did not like the way he looked at him. He also had threatened a one armed prostitute with a knife and seemed to have had blood stained hands at the time.

According to the Morning Advertiser (London) in an article on the 26th September 1888.

"Charles Ludwig, who is charged with having threatened to stab Alexander Finlay, was again brought up at the Thames Police Court yesterday, and remanded. The accused at the time he was arrested was wanted on a charge of having threatened to stab a woman in the Minores".

However he must have been innocent of the Jack the Ripper murders because he was in custody during the night of the double murder.

46. Oswald Puckridge

He was born on the 13th of June 1838 and died in 1900 and was a pharmacological chemist.

He was assumed to be a surgeon by the police and was reported to the Home Secretary for threatening people with knives.

He was committed to various asylums after August 1888 and so therefore could only have carried out the first murder, or if you include Tabram, the first two.

Therefore he is not considered a serious suspect.

47. John William Smith Sanders / Saunders

Born in 1859, he was a mad medical student.

He had the medical and geographical knowledge, but in a police report of 1st Nov 1888 he is assumed to have left the country.

He had been living at 20 Aberdeen Place, St. John's Wood, but had since left the country. A lady named Saunders resided with her son at number 20 but they left to go abroad two years ago.

He had enrolled at the London hospital Whitechapel 22nd April 1879, but ill health through over work caused his withdrawal in 1881.

One note left next to his name in the hospital register stated,

"away with Dr. Swete for several months in 1882".

He was also the superintendent in the Royal West of England sanatorium for a while.

Later in Exeter Lunatic Asylum they described his illness as a "prolonged attack of 14 years duration".

He died from heart failure, while under anaesthetic, in January 1889 aged 30. The death certificate recorded "temporarily insane". Perhaps it ran in the family as his father had killed himself in India in 1867.

Suggested as a possible suspect by Jon Ogden.

Apart from the fact that his death happened shortly after the murder of Mary Kelly there is no real supporting evidence to continue in the belief that he is a suspect.

48. Nikaner Benelius

He was a Swedish traveller arrested after walking into a woman's living room and grinning at her. He explained he wanted directions to Fenchurch Street where he was to pick up mail, but his English was not too good and anyway the door was open.

He also expressed a wish to talk to Elizabeth Stride when she was alive as her origins were Swedish too. He was released as harmless without charge.

49. Thomas John Barnardo

He was a social reformer and Irish philanthropist who was born, in Dublin, on the 4th of July 1845 and died on the 19th of September 1905.

He had met Elizabeth Stride shortly before her murder. Other than this no link can be found here.

With all the charitable works he carried out, throughout his life, this is not the character of a man who could have ever committed those atrocities.

50. L. Forbes Winslow

He was brought up in lunatic asylums as his father was a psychiatrist. He also became a psychiatrist too.

After a family feud, the running of his father's asylums was removed from his control and he altered his name. In 1888 he stated that he would use Sherlock Holmes's deductive powers and if he were given the use of six policemen he would solve the riddle of Jack the Ripper for good.

He told the Evening News dated 11th September 1888 that given the facilities he could lay hands on the maniac in a fortnight. He believed that the Canadian G. Wentworth Bell-Smith was Jack the Ripper but could not convince the police.

As for being a suspect himself, yes he was eccentric but evil, no.

At one point, hearing that Winslow was so sure of his idea of who Jack the Ripper was, Scotland Yard sent Chief Inspector Donald Swanson to interview him.

However he claimed to be not so sure as the newspapers made out and that they had misrepresented him.

51. Jill the Ripper

This theory was suggested by amongst others Arthur Conan Doyle.

The assertion being that the murders were carried out by a woman and not a man. Suggestions being,

a. Prostitute rivalry.

b. A midwife who could go round with bloodstains not calling attention to herself, or

c. A clever but mad woman for notoriety or to prove a point to friends.

Little evidence, apart from A. Crowley's essay about Blavatsky has ever been presented in connection with the Jill the Ripper theory. In 2006, analysis of the gum used on the postage stamp of one of the letters was "inconclusive" and "not forensically reliable".

An ABC TV programme Catalyst on the 30th Mar 2006 stated, after investigating the case, using a new DNA technique, one cell can produce a profile whereas conventional techniques need between 200 and 500 cells. I presume they are referring to the technique involving copying a small DNA sample until they have enough for a conclusive test. However this makes contamination errors more likely. But partial results indicated that the DNA could have been that of a woman.

Unfortunately they also took swabs from the blood on the Dear Boss letter and that was probably from the victim and not the killer. I would like to know if it was mitochondrial D.N.A. handed down from female to female through the ova or chromosomal XX D.N.A. Or she could simply lick the stamps for the Ripper totally unaware of the contents of the letters or the nature of her associate. Or the Ripper licked the stamp but was the evidence swamped by the blood DNA from the victim?

Another source claims it could only have been mitochondrial D.N.A. with only 12 mutated genes pointing to several possible men in 1890.

Another take on this theory was presented by Dr. Lawson Tait, a London surgeon. A year after the murders he put forward the theory that the murderer was an epileptic maniac who did the murders while under the influence of the fit. She would remember little of what she had done afterwards and would wash her hands and clothes. If she slaughtered animals for a living and held them from behind, slitting their throats and eviscerating them with a sharp knife, she would be so accustomed to the ritual slaughter that a murder could have happened in a semi-conscious state. The resulting wounds would point to a butcher but exhibit not much in the way of medical knowledge.

Then moving one body and leaving the others disgusted at what she had done but not able to reveal this to anyone in case she gets lynched. The fear of being caught, together with the humiliation would prevent her from revealing the truth to anyone, thus carrying the secret to her grave.

Epilepsy alone would not fully account for her actions, hence the doctor's assertion that this would have to be accompanied by some kind of mania or insane drive.

E.J. Wagner writing in the book The Science of Sherlock Holmes suggests a female suspect, Mary Pearcey.

Mary Pearcey, who had served twenty years for the murder was a convicted murderer some believe could have been Jill the Ripper.

She was born in 1866 and executed for the crime of killing her lover's wife and child on the 23rd December 1890.

She said, when questioned by the police, that she was killing mice with a poker, hence the blood spattering on her walls. The poker had actually been used to smash in the woman's skull and a knife had been used to kill the eighteen month old baby. She had dumped the body of the woman on a rubbish tip in Hampstead and the baby in a black pram a mile away.

She was 5' 6", suffered from depression and was a heavy drinker, though not an alcoholic. This seems to be a one off jealous lover's rage and does not fit any serial killer pattern, as well as the fact that women serial killers are extremely rare. I can only conclude that she was selected as a suspect in order to place at least one individual into the Jill the ripper file. Constance Kent. (born Mary Eleanor Wheeler)

Another potential Jill the Ripper could be Constance Kent (later Ruth Emilie Kaye). She was born on the 6th of February 1844 and died on the 10th April 1944.

She was suspected of killing her half-brother, three year old Francis Savill Kent. The boy was found with knife wounds on his chest and hands and his throat had been cut so deeply that the head had almost been separated.

She was arrested on the 16th of July 1860 and released without trial. She was prosecuted for the murder five years later in 1865. She had made a statement confessing her guilt to a Church of England clergyman the Rev. Arthur Wagner, and told him of her intention to give herself up to justice. She said she took the child into the privy (outside the house) and used a razor blade. It was suggested that she was mentally unbalanced.

She was at first sentenced to death but it was commuted to life in prison due to her youth at the time of her confession. Many thought she was protecting her father who was having a relationship with one of the servants and may have been caught in the act either by her or by the young boy who was going to spill the beans.

She spent the next 20 years in various prisons and was released in 1885 at the age of 41. She emigrated to Australia, trained as a nurse and worked in a school for girls from 1889 to 1909. Where was she from 1885 to 1889? Did it take her four whole years to train as a nurse?

52. Dr. John Hewitt

Born in 1850 and died in 1892, Hewitt was a suspect suggested by researcher Stewart Hicks.

He was a Manchester G.P. who became mentally ill and was sent to Coton Hill asylum in 1888.

In earlier years he was described as a young veterinary student who, according to his concerned landlady, would stay out late at night and had an obsession with the murders at the time they were committed. He had a habit of burning his clothes on those nights too. He would get the morning editions of the newspapers to read about the murders. He was also a loner who suffered from a form of insanity (general paralysis).

Soon after the murders stopped he married a nurse from the asylum and his mother and his wife took him to Bournemouth, where he died three months later. He possibly identified himself psychologically with the Ripper and the burning of the clothes were to get rid of unclean, in his mind, clothes to purify himself or remove the chance of, in his warped state of mind, being detected.

Why a G.P. would have studied to become a vet is odd. Did he change his medical direction after being a student?

53. Dr. William Evans Thomas

Born in 1856 and died in 1889. He was a Welsh Doctor with an East London practice who in 1889 committed suicide after being taken back to Anglesey from London where he poisoned himself.

He was supposed to have been in Spitalfields in the ten week killing zone but returned to visit his father after each murder. The only three links to this suspect is his medical knowledge, geographical acquaintance and ending his life after the last murders.

54. William Wescott

Born 17th Dec 1848 and died in South Africa on 30th June 1925.

He was an occultist, Freemason and co-founder of the Hermetic Order of the Golden Dawn in London.

He obtained a medical degree and became a coroner for central London and became a freemason in 1871.

Although he had the medical skills to have committed the murders, and was profoundly interested in esoteric matters there is no evidence Wescott was suspected at the time.

He had no obvious links with the Whitechapel area and was not violent or misogynistic.

55. John McCarthy

Born in Dieppe in 1851 and died in 1935.

John McCarthy was the landlord of 26 Dorset Street (13 Millers court), the address of Ripper victim Mary Kelly. He had let her rent build up to 29s. Suggestions that he may have been a regular client of Kelly's circulated.

He used a pickaxe to break down her door when an agent of his had seen the bloody mess through the broken window after being sent to collect the rent. Why did he not use his spare keys?

His assistant had already looked through the keyhole and finding it locked and with no key present, would have passed on that information unless he was too terrified by the scene past the broken window and muslin curtain and therefore did not mention the missing key.

56. Joseph Fleming

Born in 1859.

He was an ex-boyfriend of Mary Kelly. He was a stone mason-plasterer.

Fleming broke up with Kelly, possibly over her drinking but still visited even though she was living with Joseph Barnett and would bring her money.

There is a possible motive of jealousy here as it has been suggested that Kelly still had feelings for him and that they only parted because he did not like the change in personality when she had been drinking. But no motive can be found for the other murders. However according to Kelly's friend Julia Venturney he would often ill treat Kelly because she now lived with Barnett (this was before Barnett moved out of course).

57. Mr. Veck

Veck was a 'pseudo-clergyman', or one who likes to escape from buildings of poor repute dressed as a clergyman. He was actually a Post Office worker who was connected with the brothel run by Hammond.

Eventually Veck and Newlove were tried for having committed unnatural offences with male persons and having induced others to do the same.

Veck was jailed for four months and Newlove for nine. This was thought of as very unfair at the time since Veck was the worst offender and Newlove was forced to carry out various actions.

The Government was accused at the time of covering up the scandal to protect the names of any aristocratic patrons. It was rumoured that one of the brothel clients was Prince Albert Victor. However no one has yet to demonstrate the suggested connection.

58. James Hinton

Born 26th Nov 1822. Died 16th Dec 1875.

He was an English aural surgeon who died in 1875, thirteen years before the Whitechapel murders.

Because of his association with Sir William Gull he has been indirectly associated with the murders.

59. Dr. Alfred William Pearson

Pearson's handwriting is very like that found in several of the Ripper letters. He became a surgeon to the police. He was also the medical officer and public vaccinator of the Kingswinford No.3 district of the Stourbridge Union 1884 to 1920. The similarity of the handwriting to that found in two of the Ripper letters was noticed by Karen Poulin.

60. Frank Carter

Carter lived at 305 Bethnal Green Road.

His printed card was found with Catherine Eddowes after she was murdered.

Is he an independent, unconnected, person who was handing out his business cards or could it have been something more sinister? Did she have a sexual relationship with him for money or love or did she have to deal with him in some capacity or other in her daily life?

The card turned out to be P.C. Frank Carter's card given to her to reassure her about the police presence in the area and therefore no sinister overtones.

61. W.E. Gladstone

Gladstone wrote a letter about Prince Eddie but no other link can be found. He should not be considered a serious suspect.

62. Michael Kidney

Kidney was a waterside labourer who lived with 'Long Liz' Stride.

He identified her body and gave a statement stating he lived with her on and off for 5 years—except for her drunken wanderings, and that she loved him more than any other man.

His given address was 35 Dorset Street (three of the five victims also came from Dorset Street). The prostitutes may have known each other, even though there were 80,000 prostitutes (estimated) in London at that time and may have frequented the same pub, the Three Bells, on Commercial road.

Michael Kidney was not considered a suspect at the time or even now 127 years later.

63. Arbie La Bruckman

Born circa 1860

Suggested as a suspect in 2003 by Mike Conlon. This suspect was from Morocco originally. He was a cattle boat slaughterman sailing between Liverpool, London and New York for fourteen years. He was described as having a strong physique, being 5' 7" tall with dark hair and a brown moustache. He was suspected of a murder of a woman in New York but was interviewed and released. There appears to be no evidence that he was in Whitechapel at the time of the murders.

64. Charles Le Grand

Born 1853.

He had a number of aliases: Captain Anderson, Christian Briscony, Charles Grand, Charles Grant, Charles Colnette Grandy and Christian Nelson.

He was described as a Private Detective working out of 283 The Strand. He recovered the grape stalk coated with blood (which provided at least one film story line) in Dutfield's yard, which suggested that either the victim, bought some grapes from a fruit stall or was lured to her death by the same grapes.

He had a shady past and had been convicted of a series of thefts. He also sent letters demanding money from wealthy women on pain of death. He may have suffered from a mental disorder. He wandered the streets as a detective under the auspices of the Mile End Vigilance Committee. However little evidence can be collected as to any homicidal tendencies on his part. Therefore he is a weak suspect as far as I can ascertain.

65. Nicholas Vassily
(or Nicolai Wassili or Nicolai Vasiliev)

This gentleman was born in 1847 to a well off family in Titapol, Russia. He had inherited enough income to obviate the necessity for work. He was educated at Odessa University and subsequently joined a sect called the castrati or eunuchs in 1872. However, he exiled himself to France to escape persecution from the Russian Government.

He started off in a religious way searching for fallen souls he could convert or guide to a better life but soon his pattern of behaviour changed to compulsive, controlling and aggressive. He met a young woman called Madeleine and tried to alter her life style to fit his own philosophy but when she ran away, he tracked her down and stabbed her in the back. He was allegedly sent to an asylum and was released on 1st Jan 1888. Where did he go after that, London and Whitechapel? The only link to the Whitechapel murders seems to be a lot of speculation in the press. In various European newspapers carrying stories, so similar in fact that one wonders if they passed around the same rumours.

66. John Charles Netley

This suspect was born in London in 1860 and died in 1903.

He was a hackney carriage driver who was supposed to have driven the coach in which Sir William W. Gull carried out the actual killings as part of a conspiracy involving the Royal family and The Freemasons. It seems a ridiculous tale except for the assertion that Netley may have been left—handed and that according to freemasonry, a Masonic execution needed three people present and the final wound, the throat cutting to run from left to right.

However this could have been carried out by a right handed man, covering the mouth with the left hand and slitting the throat from left to right with a knife in the right hand whilst approaching quickly and quietly from behind.

67. John Avery

Avery was a misguided individual who on 12 Nov 1888, witnessed by John Carvell (a private in the 11th Hussars) confessed to having carried out the murders in a drunken state. He later apologised for the statement.

68. William Wallace Brodie

Born in 1856 he confessed to the murder of Alice McKenzie and to being Jack the Ripper. See 179

69. George Payne

ditto.

70. Dr. Tomas Dutton

This suspect lived at 130 Aldgate High Street from 1879 to 1891.

He wrote about the crimes, assisted in the post-mortems and claimed he was also a suspect. He died in abject poverty. He would have had both the medical knowledge as well as skills in dissection and would have known the area very well.

71. Ernest Dowson

Dowson was born on 2nd August 1867 and became a poet.

Suggestions from a 1935 writer called Hopkins (who called him Mr. Moring) taken up recently by Martin Fido who both suggested that he was seen with Mary Kelly before she was murdered.

He fitted witness George Hutchingson's original description of the man in question.

Dowson did live in the Whitechapel area at that time but was supposedly a drug addict so there is little reason to think of him as a suspect.

72. Timothy Donovan (i)

Donovan worked as a labourer who was 28 years of age at the time and knew Annie Chapman. He died from cirrhosis of the liver and exhaustion on 1st Nov 1888. Interesting as a suspect except for the fact that Donovan died before Mary Kelly's Murder.

73. Timothy Donovan (ii)

However there is a second Timothy Donovan aged 30 at the time and in 1904 murdered his wife. He had a history of violence and was alive during the ripper's spree and would have been very familiar with the local geography.

74. Joseph Denny

Denny was another suspect who fitted George Hutchinson's description of the man seen with Mary Kelly shortly before she was murdered. He was therefore reported to police on 28th December 1888. He subsequently managed to prove he was at a different location at the time of the murder.

75. John Davidson

His real name was John George Donkin who trained as a doctor and then served two prison terms for assaults on women.

However even though he sported a moustache and was within the height range in the ripper's profile he could prove he was not at the addresses on the dates of the murders and was exonerated of all suspicion.

76. George Cullen alias Squibby

Born in 1863, Cullen was a 25 year old muscle man and street gambler who came to the attention of the police when he threw a stone at a policeman and it struck a young girl. He was chased and onlookers shouted "Jack the Ripper" and surrounded the police station. He was later released, when the hysterical crowd dispersed and was subsequently handed a three month prison sentence.

In the 1930's an author Benjamin Leeson stated that Squibby had been charged with various knife crimes.

No link to the Ripper apart from the imaginings of a hysterical mob.

77. Douglas Cow

This suspect was almost an example of hysteria.

He was reported on 21st Nov 1888 by Fanny Drake of looking like the description of the Whitechapel murderer after she became alarmed and anxious when he kept grinning at her. The suspect was interviewed and was found to be respectable in appearance and was immediately released without charge.

78. James Connell

An Irishman born in 1852, he took Martha Spencer for a walk in Hyde Park and made her anxious and uncomfortable when he started talking about Jack the Ripper and asylums. She took her suspicions to the police and he was taken to Hyde Park police station on 22nd Nov 1888 but could prove his address and that he was a decent man. He was released without charge.

79. George Robert Gissing

Gissing was an English novelist, born in Wakefield 22nd Nov 1857.

He was caught stealing money from a cloakroom for prostitute Nell Harrison, whom he later married and eventually paid her to leave him as she was often drunk and returned to prostitution.

He married his second wife Edith Underwood in 1891 and moved to Exeter.

He left for Italy on 16th Sept 1888 and was still there during the Ripper murders, so not considered a suspect.

80. Pastor John George Gibson

Gibson was named as Jack the Ripper by author Robert Graysmith in the book The Bell Tower. He suggests that Theo Durrant, a 24 year old medical student, who was arrested, found guilty and executed on 7th Jan 1898 for the murder of two women, Blanch Lamont 18 and Minnie Williams 21, in San Francisco's Baptist church, was innocent and that the real culprit was Gibson, the church pastor. John George Gibson was born in Edinburgh on 14th August 1859 and at the time of the Ripper murders would have been 29. He was 5' 9" tall with a small sandy moustache. He was supposed to have confessed to the two murders on his death bed but to whom did he confess? Also he appears to have been serving in a church in Scotland at the time of Jack the Ripper's rampage. It is also worthwhile pointing out that he is a little too tall, at 5' 9" to fit the profile.

81. William John Foster

On the 11th October 1888 Foster was arrested (in bed at the time they called) at 11 Memel street Belfast on information received. The policeman described his occupation as a watchmaker but Foster said he had an allowance, from his father who was a rich brewer, and therefore did not have to work.

He was connected to Greenock, Glasgow and Edinburgh and had bloody razors in his bag. Apart from the latter piece of information I cannot see why he was a Ripper suspect. It is easy to cut your face shaving with a razor.

82. John Fitzgerald

A plasterer-bricklayer's labourer, confessed to a member of the public that he had committed the Annie Chapman murder. The police found out that he had been drinking for several days and actually had an alibi for the date of her murder. So there at least two reasons to exclude him from the possible genuine suspect list.

83. William Alfred Field

Field was a sixty year old gardener who was charged with being drunk and disorderly between one and two in the morning of Saturday 24th November 1888. He had scared various women by chasing them shouting 'I'm Jack the ripper'. Not a suspect as aggression and bravado are both magnified by alcohol consumption.

84. Collingwood Hilton Fenwick

According to a headline 'The Spitalfields Murder' in the Daily News edition of 16th November 1888, it was reported that one

"Collingwood Hilton Fenwick, a young man in a good social position, was brought before Mr. Lade at the Southwark Police Court yesterday for cutting and wounding Ellen Worsfold at Ann's-place, Waterloo road."

He was remanded. A one off crime does not make Jack the Ripper.

85. Frank Edwards

In 1959 a retired blacksmith told this story to the newspapers:

'In 1888, shortly after the double murder of Stride and Eddowes he visited his cousin in West Sussex (Frank Edwards) he noticed a blood-stained shirt collar and razor in his attaché case. He concluded 70 years later that he must be Jack the Ripper'

However it is more likely that his cousin was embarrassed that he had cut himself while shaving.

86. W.H. Eaton

A member of the public who wrote to the Star newspaper, Saturday 10th November 1888 edition, and lived at 22 Fonthill road, Finsbury stated that he was interested in visiting the locale of the Dorset Street murder.

A crowd sprung up calling him 'Jack the Ripper' and so he gave himself up to the custody of a constable at the Bishopsgate station.

The officers were satisfied that he had done nothing wrong and was released. This incident, portrayed in the letter to the press, just shows how the hysterical mob scene could be fired up, in that area and at that time by even an innocent curiosity.

87. William James

James was a 33 year old hawker who was charged with the manslaughter of William Hall whom he had claimed was making improper advances to a married woman he was with. He claimed he only shoved him—but he later died from his injuries.

It was only when he called himself Jack the Ripper to a policeman, who did not take him seriously, that he is considered a suspect. A sick joke does not make one guilty of the atrocities.

88. Henry James

James was a well known local lunatic who was accused of being Jack the Ripper by a railway signalman who saw him behaving oddly, as if he had one stiff arm and Thomas Ede also reported he had seen the suspect with a knife. He was questioned and cleared of suspicion. There was no suggestion the knife was used to stab or mutilate women.

89. Joseph Isaacs

Isaacs was born in 1858 and was a thirty year old Polish / Jewish cigar maker at the time of the murders. He threatened violence to any woman over the age of 17 and was reported to the police. However, they could only charge him with the theft of a watch from a pawnshop.

90. Benjamin Isaacs

An omnibus conductor told of a man, who, after getting on at Highgate announced that he was Jack the Ripper and threatened to knife one of the female passengers. He was ordered to leave the bus and was immediately arrested. He was later shown to be one Ben Isaacs who was forty years of age. He was later charged with disorderly conduct. A lot of attention seekers, at that time, wanted to be known as Jack the Ripper—it probably added a little spice to their lives.

91. Jack Irwin

This suspect was suggested by A.H.Skirving of the Canadian police as the Ripper. He was a prisoner in Ontario. Subsequent investigations showed he was not in England at the time of the Whitechapel slayings.

92. William Holt

Holt was a doctor at St. George's hospital who thought of himself as a bit of a detective. Under various disguises he patrolled the streets of the East End hoping to trap Jack the Ripper. On the 11th November, two days after the murder of Mary Kelly he did the same again having covered his face with burnt cork (as they do in the army). His odd appearance frightened a woman in George yard, almost the same place where Martha Tabram had been murdered. A lynch mob surrounded him and next day he was arrested and proved his innocence of the murders.

93. Alfred Hinde

Hinde was a watchmaker who was briefly suspected of being Jack the ripper when a policeman who saw him defending a woman against an assault assumed he was the aggressor. Witnesses came forward to clear him.

94. John Hill

Hill was a 31 year old ship's fireman was charged with assault and intent to ravish Elizabeth Tilley. This took place in Old Brunswick Road on the 10th March 1891 at 9 p.m. He told the woman Jack had got her. Sentencing was prorogued until medical officers had examined him.

95. George Richard Henderson

Henderson was charged in October 1888 with loitering about the streets and had a black bag with him. Witnesses came forward to clear his name.

96. Julius Lippman

Died in 1900. He was another person who was nicknamed Leather Apron and he came to the attention of the police in 1889. He was a cobbler and satisfied the police of his innocence. The psychological pressure of guilt by association and a decline in his trade drove him to drink and he died from self-neglect and starvation.

97. Wolf Levisohn

While on business in Whitechapel on 15th November 1888 Levisohn was accosted by two well-known prostitutes who solicited him. When he refused their advances they shouted 'you are Jack the Ripper'. They later reported him because he looked like the description of the Ripper and carried a shiny black bag. Interviewed by inspector Abberline he stated that Klosowski was not the Ripper and that he should investigate a Russian barber's assistant in Walworth Road about the Whitechapel murders. Dismissed by the police at the time Levisohn was suggested as an accomplice of Jack the Ripper by author Michael Gordon.

98. Henry Edward Leeke

An unfortunate man of small stature who was assumed to be Jack the Ripper and dragged from a pub at 5 p.m. down the street to the magistrate by two men pretending to be detectives. All he was doing to attract attention was talking to himself.

99. John Leary

Leary was a soldier spoken to by a policeman at 2a.m. on the night that Martha Tabran was murdered on 7th August 1888. He was asked why he was loitering and told the constable that he was waiting for a mate who had gone with a girl. As Tabram was estimated to have been murdered at 2.30 a.m. it became of extreme importance to trace this soldier. An identification parade was held and Constable Barrett was told to be careful, when he attempted to pick out the individual due to the importance of the correct identification of the suspect. He subsequently picked out Leary who was able to prove that he was with Private Law, who corroborated his statement.

100. Jose Laurenco

Born in 1862 it was suggested, by a customs clerk, that Laurenco should be a suspect since the injuries inflicted by The Ripper were similar to those inflicted by Portuguese peasants on the French during the Peninsular war. Hence, the clerk concluded that it was a Portuguese sailor.

However, Laurenco had not been on the City Of Cork ship when it docked on 8th Nov 1888, so he was not in London when Mary Kelly was murdered.

The customs clerk mentioned above suggested five people. Four who were supposed to have worked together in order to carry out the crimes. All five were exonerated. Being a customs clerk he would not have been charged with wasting police time.

101. John Langhorn

Langhorn was a crank who in Montreal assaulted a Miss Florrie Newcomb. Two men heard the screams and detained him. When in custody he claimed he was Jack the Ripper and that he had carried out fifteen murders in the Whitechapel area.

He had a letter with him which he had signed Jack the Ripper, a large knife and 25 cents.

He wished to be arrested and hung and was 4' 6" tall. The local newspapers also claimed he was a well known liar although he did have a cockney accent.

Far too short to be considered as a suspect. Another attention seeker.

102. John Lagan

The British Consul in Boulogne wrote to the police with his suspicions of a man called John Lagan. He had asked the consul for
some assistance to go to Cardiff to work in the coal mines. He originally worked in America but also had taken lodgings in Hamilton
near Glasgow.

He had fitted the recent drawing of the Ripper which had
appeared in the Daily Telegraph on the 6th October 1888. He was,
however later cleared of any involvement with the Whitechapel
murders.

103. Vassily Konovalov. Aliases Alexei Pedachenko and Andrey Luiskovo

This suspect who was born in 1857 and died in 1908 was a junior
surgeon from Russia who in 1887 murdered a woman in Paris then
the five prostitutes in Whitechapel and then another woman in
Russia in 1891. This appears to be a variation of the Russian spy
theory i.e. a man who was supposedly sent to discredit London
police. This suspect was proposed by Donald McCormick in 1959.
I just do not believe any of it.

104. Bertram Knutson

On the 8th October 1888 a man who was seen sleeping rough and
begging in Eltham disturbed some locals. He especially disturbed
the women who thought he might be Jack the Ripper. The police
went looking for him and one Inspector Harris found him asleep
and covered in grass. He turned out to be a 23 year old Norwegian
sailor. The police court directed the police to take him to the
workhouse.

105. James Johnson

Johnson was interviewed after a prostitute, Elizabeth Hudson,
stated he had asaulted her at two in the morning and carried a large
knife. He stated that he pushed her to the ground after she had
put her hand in his pocket looking for money and that he carried

no knife. He was a waiter with an American accent. The police put it down to a bad scrape with a well-known and troublesome prostitute.

106. Antoni Pricha

Born circa 1858.

It was after George Hutchinson gave his detailed description of The Ripper suspect seen with Mary Kelly shortly before her death, that Edward Night Larkin saw Pricha, and informed the police that he fitted the same description. He was questioned and soon proved his innocence. Probably the fact that he had a long brown astrakhan-trimmed overcoat induced Larkin to become suspicious.

107. William Henry Piggot

Piggot, then aged 52 was arrested while carrying a bundle of shirts with blood on them and he had blood spatters on his shoes. He claimed a prostitute bit his hand. He had also been doing some heavy drinking. He had (according to a reporter from the Echo) an iron-grey beard. Released without charge. His story seemed to check out.

108. John Benjamin Perryman a.k.a 'The mad barber of Pekham'.

Perryman was a 40 year old hairdresser, and on the 14th November 1888, had got drunk and manhandled several women. He also had a black bag and carried a dagger. A crowd gathered proclaiming he was Jack the Ripper and became quite vociferous. The police, with difficulty, because of the crowd, took him to the police station. There they found a dagger and a sheath. He said he was going to get it ground but had also been drinking and events had gone out of control. He is not regarded as a serious suspect.

109. Alfred Pearson

Pearson, a moulder was charged with threatening a couple while out walking. He was supposed to have flashed a big weapon and added the words 'Jack the Ripper'. He was bound over for six months but the weapon turned out to be a trowel.

110. Alfred Parent

Alfred Parent, a French man and another resident at Bacon's hotel Fitroy square came under suspicion on 15th Nov 1888 when, instead of offering sixpence in exchange for sex, he offered one sovereign for sex and five sovereigns to spend the night with him. The girl, Annie Cook became frightened, since as she put it, he could 'want to take me into a room and murder me'.

However he was able to prove to the police that he was not in the Whitechapel area during the times of the murders and after being questioned he was released.

111. Dr. Dimitru Panchenko

This doctor was notorious for supplying cholera and diphtheria bacteria to a man who wanted to kill his wealthy parents. In 1911 he was sent to jail for 15 years for his part in the crime. No link was ever found, however, between this doctor and the Whitechapel murders. The whole case seems to rest on three sets of faked documents.

112. Augustus Nochild

Known also as August, Nochild was a 52 year old tailor of Christian Street, Whitechapel. He assaulted a prostitute, Sarah McFarly on the morning of the 2nd October 1888, just after half past twelve. He had asked her to go with him to his house and stated that if she did not 'I will murder you if you don't. I have murdered women in Whitechapel, and I would like to do another'.

Police sergeant Perry saw him grab her by the throat. She cried out 'police' and 'murder' and Nochild was immediately arrested. The officer noticed that both individuals appeared to be under the influence of drink and Mr. Alderman Stone did not think there was any basis for a charge, and dismissed the case. Drunken boasting together with spurious claims do not constitute a case for a Ripper suspect.

113. Thomas Murray

Thomas Murray was admitted to an asylum on the 8th June 1889. He was thirty years old, single and with no occupation. Sexual and alcoholic excesses were given as reasons for his insanity. He had thrown furniture, was very violent and had made death threats against both his sister and mother. He was paranoid and heard voices. He had threatened children in the street who were constantly chanting 'Jack the Ripper' at him. This information was researched in the London Metropolitan archives by one Robert W. House. Alcoholism and insanity together with threats against family and children do not make a convincing case for a Jack the Ripper suspect. After all he did not stab or cut either his mother or sister and never physically harmed the taunting children.

114. Thomas Murphy

On the 13th November 1888 a search of the casual wards in Holborn, by the police, produced a suspect who gave his name as Thomas Murphy. A search of his person revealed a knife with a blade of about 10" in length. It was established that he was a sailor and could prove he was in another place at the time of the Whitechapel murders.

115. Joseph Woods

After the murder of Annie Chapman streetwalkers were told you will either be arrested or can carry a whistle. So a young prostitute called Eleanor Candy took a whistle with her. She picked up an 18 year old, drunken Joseph Woods shortly after midnight in Commercial Street. He told her, after he found out she had a whistle, that he had a knife and was Jack the ripper. She blew her whistle and Woods was arrested for indecent assault. Too young to be the ripper according to the widely held profile at the time.

116. James Wilson

On Tuesday 27th November 1888, just after twelve noon a man was pursued by an angry mob calling out 'Jack the Ripper' through the streets of Belfast. He took refuge in a house and two policemen searched the property. He was arrested and turned out to be a 43 year old ballad singer / comedian. He was arrested for his own protection and is and was no suspect.

117. Frederick White

Aged 42 and described as a commission agent, White threatened a woman at a train station saying 'I will rip you up, I am Jack the Ripper, if I don't do it now, I shall know you again' all the while trying to trip her up. He produced a rambling statement of why he did this and was fined 10s and released.

118. William Waddell

In the evening of 22nd September 1888 in Birttley Fell, County Durham, the body of a young woman was found in a field. Her throat had been cut and her intestines were protruding. She was identified as 28 year old Jane Beetmoor. Due to the mutilations this crime was, in the first instance, linked to the Ripper murders. A young labourer, William Waddell came under suspicion as he was seen with Jane on the night of her murder. He had fled the district and had exchanged his blood stained clothes for those of a lower value. He was arrested, found guilty and hanged at Durham prison on 18th December 1888. Inspector Roots and Dr. Phillips travelled to the North of England to investigate the claims of a link to the Whitechapel murders and satisfied themselves that it was a local incident.

119. Nicholai Van Burst

Nicholi Van Burst was a Dutchman living in a hotel in Fitzroy square. He accosted several women at Kings Cross station on the evening of 25th Nov 1888. He had good alibis and in any case was too old and too tall to be the Ripper as he was 50 years old and 5' 11" tall.

120. Emil Totterman (alias Carl Nielson)

Born between 1862 and 1868.

In 1903 a Finnish sailor was arrested for the murder of prostitute Sarah Martin. He was sentenced to life in prison he would have been 20 years old in 1888. Too young perhaps to fit the profile of Jack the Ripper? He was also released from prison, in recognition of his heroic naval services during the Spanish-American war and returned to Finland in 1929.

121. A monkey

A woman living on the Isle of Wight suggested this one. She thought it might be a large ape which could have escaped from a wild beast show. No further comment required.

122. Charles Thomas

Thomas was a labourer who made a drunken claim on 12th Jan 1888 in front of a crowd of "I'm Jack the Ripper". This got him 15 days hard labour. Not a serious suspect.

123. Lewis Stemler

Born circa 1884.

Lewis was a 29 year old out of work Austrian waiter who was suspected of being Jack the Ripper after he was accused of frightening a group of five and six year old boys and chasing them along First Avenue, New York.

Feelings were running high as a young boy, Charlie Murray had been murdered (and had lived on First Avenue). Also a letter had been received by the boy's mother that he would murder another child as soon as all the excitement had died down. No link has yet to be found, however, with Stemler and Jack the Ripper in London.

Also if one takes care to assess his date of birth in connection with the Whitechapel murders one soon realises that he would have to have been approximately four years old at the time—an amazing feat.

124. Louis Solomon

Solomon was mentioned in Home Office files. Officers at Woking prison sent a letter dated 15th Nov 1888 which suggested that the murderer Solomon may be Jack the Ripper. The letter was destroyed after its receipt had been recorded. A case of now suspecting any murderer?

125. John Brinckly

On 14th Nov 1888 a 40 year old porter of Wilmington place, when drunk, claimed that he was Jack the Ripper. Again a drunken claim.

126. John Brennan

Immediately after the Annie Chapman murder a 39 year old drunken Irishman called John Brennan burst into the White Hart public house in Southampton Street, Camberwell and shouted out that leather apron was a friend of his and that he had the murder weapon in his pocket. This cleared the pub and after terrorising the landlady (who locked herself in a room in the pub to get away from him until the police arrived) constable Pillow arrived and found his mood had changed, from the stories he had heard and that he (Brennan) considered it only a joke.

127. Samuel Augustus Barnett

Barnett and his wife were merely social commentators and letter writers about social conditions at the time of the murders—no suspect here.

128. Daniel Barnett

Older brother of main suspect Joseph Barnett. He visited Mary Kelly the day before she was murdered. Possibly trying to get her to understand Joseph better? Perhaps he was trying to get them together again and suggesting to Mary that she stops putting up prostitutes in her apartment because the rent would go up and she would be tempted to go back on the streets again with a friend in the same oldest profession? There appears to be little chance of him being a true suspect.

129. Sir George Arthur

Arthur was a soldier and an actor. When he was 28 he liked to slum it, as many rich Victorians liked to do, but chose Whitechapel at the time of the murders to do this. He was arrested when he talked to a well-known prostitute, and because he fitted the popular description of J.T.R. He soon proved his innocence however and embarrassing headlines were to follow.

130. John Arnold—A.K.A. John Cleary, John Leary, John Kemp or Denis Lynch.

This suspect posed as a detective to reporters claiming that there was a torso of a mutilated woman and was there a reward. He did not take them to the exact spot but told them where it was. When no body was discovered it was thought of as another crank. However two days later a human torso was discovered in that spot. He predicted (or was connected with) the Pinchin Street torso murder. Possibly he was between 25-28 years of age and of average height but other descriptions vary. Certainly an interesting suspect if the torso case connects with the Whitechapel series of Jack the Ripper murders. Otherwise not a suspect.

131. Frederico Albericci

An Italian-American who was a footman who was called Frederick by employer Sir William Gull. He was supposedly part of the Masonic conspiracy theory. Not considered a legitimate suspect.

132. Claude Reignier Conder

Colonel Conder was not suspected at the time of the murders but recent research by crime writer Tom Slemen and criminologist Keith Andrews suggest that a 39 year old British intelligence officer, archaeologist, writer, map-maker, and trained killer was Jack the Ripper.

It has been suggested that artefacts and rings excavated by Conder and Sir Charles Warren, from King Solomon's temple in Jerusalem, were stolen from his home by Annie Chapman. Perhaps a bit too wild a theory but if Warren was earlier associated with the archaeologist then perhaps events could have been hushed up obliterating the link between the colonel and the crimes?

133. Frank Casellano

Newspaper reports from the Mountain Democrat on 1st April 1893 stated that the New York police have Jack the Ripper in custody. The story goes that a man ripped up the side of a woman on March 19th in New York leaving the large bladed knife in the wound. The knife was traced to one Frank Castellano who the police were already interested in. He was an Italian barber and a short while earlier had worked as a fireman on one of the Trans-Atlantic steamers.

Links were made, as well, to the murder of Carrie Brown on 24th April 1891 as he may have been the mysterious man who was with her when they went to the East River Hotel on the night of her murder. However it does not sound like Jack the Ripper's profile and he would never leave a knife in the body of the victim even if in a hurry.

134. Edwin Burrows

This individual was a vagrant and was arrested on the 8th December 1888 because he was wearing a peaked cap described by Israel Schwartz who had witnessed Elizabeth Stride being thrown to the ground by a man wearing a similar cap before she was murdered. Not displaying enough purpose in his life to be considered a candidate for the role of Jack the Ripper in any scenario perhaps?

135. Hans Bure

In October 1888 a well-dressed German man was charged with assaulting one Elizabeth Jennings at 12.30 on a Saturday night. He said 'come with me' trying to drag her. When the crowd nearby heard the screams they became hostile and chanted Jack the Ripper. Through an interpreter in the local police station he said sorry but that he had thought she was a prostitute. He also stated that he had been drinking. His sentence was either a fine of 40s or one month hard labour.

136. William Bull

Bull was born in 1861 and was 27 years of age at the time of the Ripper spree. He lived at 6 Stannard Road, Dalton. He walked into Bishopgate police station on 5th October 1888 and promptly confessed to the murder of Catherine Eddowes. He also related to the police that he was a medical student at the London hospital. A check with the hospital produced the interesting fact that he did not work there. He was subsequently found to be unemployed and made the confession when drunk. His family was contacted and said that he was in bed asleep when that murder took place. With that alibi established, what looked like a wonderful stroke of luck turned into another example of an attention seeking individual. It was not surprising that he had claimed that he had thrown the clothing he had been wearing that night into 'the Lea' and the knife he apparently threw away also, very convenient.

137. Edward Buchan

Buchan was born on 19th November 1859 and lived at 37 Robin Hood Lane, a distance of three miles from Whitechapel. He was a shoemaker and store dealer who killed himself by cutting his throat on the day of Mary Kelly's funeral in 1888. Apparently he had been behaving oddly for several weeks. This sounds very much like developing schizophrenia. He was 29 years of age. There is no link—apart from the coincidental date, between him and Jack the Ripper.

138. Peter J. Harpick

This suspect proposed by author Jonathan Goodman in a book entitled 'Who he' in 1984. Since this is an obvious anagram of Jack the Ripper, there is no point in dealing with this invented suspect.

139. James Hardiman

Hardiman was suggested in 2004 as a suspect by Robert Hills.

He was born in Mile end, Whitechapel, before July 1845 or 1858, or the 12 of October 1859, at 31 The High Street, Mile End, New Town in the registration district of Whitechapel. He was the fourth son of Samuel and Sarah (or Harriet) Hardiman. His mother sold cat meat and pieces of horse flesh.

He was 43(or 29) at the time of the murders. His daughter died from syphilis and his wife died on 15th September 1888. He died from consumption (tuberculosis). He hated all mothers and he may have been avenging his daughter's death who inherited syphilis from her mother, his wife. He knew the local area and could use a knife.

Adrian Stockton claims 'My first cousin three times removed was Jack the Ripper—now that's something to talk about'.

On the 8th of September 1888 Annie Chapman's mutilated body was found in the back yard of his mother's house. Although he lived at 29 Hanbury Street at one time James resided at 13 Heneage Street at the time of this Ripper murder.

A suspect worth further investigation, perhaps, particularly as there is a later date of birth recorded and a statement that he died aged 32. A little difficult to die aged 32 when he could have been 43 at the time of the murders.

There appear to be three sets of biographical data here two cannot be correct. Either there are three men called James Hardiman in the area (we know that there were two individuals called Joseph Barnett in Dorset Street at the time) or errors have been made.

The Ripperologist magazine believes this suspect to be Jack the Ripper. Two alleged Ripper letters talk of a horse slaughterer and Joe the cats meats man, is this the same person? Were they written by the Ripper? Or were these hoaxes or more red herrings? Research by Robert Hills seems to be on the right track. He died in 1891 according to the Complete Jack the Ripper A to Z (2010).

Theophill Hanhart—Born in 1864 the son of a German pastor, Hanhart taught French and German at a high school near Bath. Then he suddenly claimed he was Jack the ripper. Inspector Reid satisfied himself that he could not have committed the crimes and

Hanhart was adjudged to be suffering from mental derangement and not fit to be allowed into the community. He was sent to Shoreditch infirmary. The Morning Advertiser(London) dated 24th December 1888 ran with the story that a policeman saw him wandering up and down a road and when asked what was wrong he claimed that he had the Whitechapel murders on his conscience and that a knife in his possession was the murder weapon. He was arrested and it transpired that his odd behaviour had forced a friend to move him to London for a change of scene but that he had disappeared until he was arrested. A Rev. W. Mathias stated that he had taught at his college and that overwork had possibly brought about his condition and delusions. So it would appear that his state of mind could not have allowed him to carry out this string of murders.

140. Edward Hambler

In October 1889 a ship's joiner was arrested for causing affray and being dressed as a woman. 600 people, who suspected him to be Jack the Ripper or wanted to mock him had him surrounded. The court bound him over to keep the peace, fined him ten pounds sterling and suggested that he did not look very attractive as a woman anyway, to great amusement among the spectators in the court.

141. William Griffiths

William went up to a police officer, on the 10th October 1888, in Essex road, and claimed that he was Jack the Ripper and produced a large penknife. Finding the man to be drunk the officer took him to the police station where he admitted 'it was a drunken freak'. He was charged with being drunk and disorderly. Another example of drunken daring do.

142. Alfred Gray

Gray was an English tramp arrested in Tunis in 1889 with a gang of burglars and suspected of being J.T.R. simply because he came from Spitalfields. While he was being interviewed they noticed the tattoo of a naked woman on his arm. Drink and a love of women alone do not make for a good Jack the Ripper suspect.

143. William Grant Grainger

A 28 year old man at the time of the Ripper murders (as he was 41 years old in the 1901 census). He was born in Cork in 1860, allegedly trained for the medical profession, then joined the Cork city artillery. However he was dismissed, as being of bad character, in 1889. He spent the next few years wandering between Cork and London.

He was caught by police in March 1895 in the Spitalfields area, after he had stabbed a prostitute in the abdomen claiming her price was excessive. Alice Graham was the lady of the streets. He was sentenced to 10 years and released in 1902 after serving seven. It was reported that he had claimed to be Jack the Ripper in prison. Was he in Whitechapel in 1888? Why did he let the prostitute cry out? This is not the style of Jack the ripper, hand over mouth first and then cut the throat, is more J.T.R's M.O.

144. Benjamin Graham

Graham was a 42 year old glassblower of Fletcher's row and was arrested on the 17th October 1888 and taken to Snow Hill police station after confessing to the Whitechapel murders when drunk. He was released without charge.

According to a newspaper report from the Eastern Post & City Chronicle dated Saturday 27th October 1888, Mr. Alderman Renals had remanded him for a week while a doctor's report into his state of mind could be prepared and it stated (as read by the chief clerk) that the prisoner had suffered through excessive drinking. Mr Renals regretted that he could not charge the prisoner as he had caused the police a lot of trouble.

145. James Green x 2

Two people of the same name both suspects by association only.

The first James Green washed blood from the street after the murder of Mary Ann Nichols. The second attended the inquest of Annie Chapman and lived at 36 Action Street, he also went to the assistance of John Davis, who had found the body of Annie Chapman. The address of the first James Green was New Cottage

2 Bucks row. Both characters seem to have been fused together into one suspect by certain writers.

146. James Monro

Monro was an Edinburgh born detective whom an Australian author believes could have been a suspect and had a pathological hatred of Sir Charles Warren. I cannot find any evidence to uphold this claim.

147. Frank Miles

Miles was a colour blind painter who was suggested as a suspect by Thomas Toughill. However in 1881 he had a nervous breakdown and by 1887 his mental health had deteriorated so much that he was confined to Brislington asylum near Bristol. He stayed there until his death on 15th June 1894.

Very little chance of him being the Ripper—too unstable. Also the security in such an establishment would not allow him to have slipped in and out without being noticed.

148. Edward Mc Kenna

He was arrested on 14th September 1888 after threatening to stab people. He sold laces, boxes and purses for a living and his pockets bore this out (together with one spring onion). He is not considered as a serious suspect.

149. Joseph Carey Merrick

Born 1862. Died 1890.

This man, who suffered from proteus syndrome (more commonly known as the elephant man), was a gentle, kind soul who had an unfortunate history because of his disfigurement caused by a genetic growth disorder. He was exhibited, for a while, at the back of a shop on Whitechapel road opposite the London Hospital. In the same shop in 1888 a minor businessman was putting on a display of amateur wax effigies of the victims of Jack the Ripper. No one could possibly link this tragic, empathic figure to the Ripper murders. That which scares ignorant people sometimes makes them think the worst. An uglier side of the hysteria at that time (no pun intended).

150. Jack McCurdy

On the first day of December 1888 the chief of police of Minneapolis received a letter from one William Halen alias Knife Stab, late of London, England. Together with threats it stated that he was a pal of Jack McCurdy alias Jack the Ripper. Was this a hoax letter? The ramblings of a deranged mind or crank? Or a prank?

151. Oliver Matthews

Matthews possessed a small black bag which made another man suspicious which prompted him to report him to the police. The police questioned him and searched his bag, finding only linen, and coupled with the fact that Mr. Matthews was able to prove his innocence, was released without charge.

152. Thomas Mason

A newspaper reported on 28th April 1895 that Medium Robert Lees had had a psychic impression of the Whitechapel murderer and had traced him to an asylum in Islington where he found a mad doctor called Thomas Mason but who was recognised by others as Gull, the famous doctor, who had presumably gone insane. Gull's heart gave him problems, together with a stroke not his sanity. As for the real Thomas Mason, he was a 71 year old retired bookbinder from Islington and had never set foot inside an asylum in his life.

153. Arthur Henry Mason

In a Scotland Yard file, dated 18th December 1888 Mason's strange behaviour at the White Hart public house was noted because it caused suspicion. He also fitted the popular description of Jack the Ripper found in newspapers. He was interviewed by the police and released.

154. Richard Mansfield

Mansfield was an American actor, even though he was actually born in Helgoland, Germany, on the 24th May 1857.

At the time of the Ripper murders he was acting at the Lyceum Theatre in a production of Robert Lewis Stevenson's Dr. Jekyll and Mr. Hyde. He became a suspect, in the popular imagination, because of his convincing transformation into Mr. Hyde on stage. It might incite murder, was the odd belief. They did not know about pre-painted faces, colour filters, altering shadows and grease paint. One for the realms of Ripper mythology I think.

155. John Lock

On Wednesday 3rd October 1888 on Ratcliff Highway there was a report that a man had been seen behaving in an odd way and he had blood stains on his coat. A crowd gathered and started chanting 'leather apron' and 'Jack the Ripper'. The man fearing for his safety took shelter in the Victory public house. When a policeman arrived it was discovered that he was a navy reserve sailor and the so-called blood stains were in fact paint and grease stains. Yet another hysterical over reaction.

156. Henry Skinnerton

On 21st October 1888 Henry Skinnerton, a 50 year old labourer was charged with assault and breaking 25 panes of glass worth £1. He had grabbed a man called Corney by the throat and after proclaiming that he was Jack the Ripper and had also carried out a murder in Hatton gardens, he ran away. Corney and a friend chased him and Skinnerton jumped onto a lean to and here is where the glass was broken. He was fined £1 and 12s, which included costs. However no one thinks he could have been the Ripper, just a case of booze induced aggression release and attention seeking daring do.

157. George Robert Sims

A journalist who wrote about the murders and claimed that in 1888 a coffee stall holder in Whitechapel saw a portrait of Simms advertising his latest book and believed he resembled the suspicious man with bloodstained cuffs who had come to his stall shortly after the double murder. Sims also thought he himself looked like the descriptions of Jack the Ripper. Sims came to believe that the Ripper was Montague John Drewitt. In 1913, to counter these rumours, Inspector John Littlechild wrote to Sims naming Dr. Tumblety as a better suspect. This was subsequently known as the Littlechild letter.

158. Clarence Simm

On the 20th June 1989 an article appeared in the Weekly World News in which a widow called Betty Simm claimed that her late husband Clarence had made a deathbed confession to her in 1951. He had told her that as a teenager he had killed 14 prostitutes, to free them from a life of sin. No description of Jack the Ripper sounds like a teenager. Also that is a lot of Jack the Ripper murders and it would have to include several either side of the usual accepted 5 to make any sense and that still would not explain those murders which involved more than one person, which you would need to include, to make up the numbers.

159. James Shaw (Pennock)

Arrested on suspicion of being the murderer, James Pennock and had a copy of the illustrated Whitechapel murders in his pocket. However the original murderer, they were looking for, was two inches smaller and this suspect had a sebaceous cyst the size of a walnut on his head together with an obvious scar. No link was found either with Pennock or with the Whitechapel murders and he was released without charge.

160. Reginald Saunderson

Saunderson was linked to a murder of a woman in Kensington on the night of the 25th November 1894. However similar the murder was to the ripper's M.O. (her throat had been cut) he would have been 15 years old at the time of the Whitechapel murders. So I discount him as a valid suspect.

161. John Royall

In July 1889 a 35 year old labourer was charged with violently assaulting and threatening to murder one Nora Brown. He threatened to 'rip her' and she told a police officer that she suspected him of being Jack the Ripper. He claimed that he was drunk and it was a mistake. However the police officer who arrested him thought he acted in quite a sober manner. He was remanded in custody. Sounds like someone just chancing his arm and not a valid contender for the man who deserved the epithet Jack the Ripper.

162. Pierce John Robinson

Born in 1854, Robinson was a tall man with a dark beard who was once jailed for a short while for bigamy. Other reports suggest he was a religious fanatic and a Baptist. He came under suspicion from his business partner who was a baker. He went quiet whenever the Whitechapel murders were brought up in conversation and in a letter to a female friend he stated his fear that he would 'be caught today'. He had medical training too. However the woman to whom he wrote the letter gave him an alibi for the day of the Mary Kelly murder (although alibis from girlfriends are a little suspicious).

163. John Richardson

Richardson was working as a porter at Spitalfields market. He was on his way to work at 4.45 a.m. on Saturday 8th September 1888, when he called in at 29 Hanbury Street to check the locks on the yard where his mother ran her business. Everything appeared normal and he paused to trim a piece of leather from his boot which was making it painful to walk. John Davis, while on his way to work discovered the mutilated body of Annie Chapman, just yards from where Richardson had claimed to have sat only one hour before. Richardson also claimed he could easily see round the yard and, that at that time, it was empty. When it was learned that he carried a knife and a leather apron belonging to him had been found under a tap in the yard he came under suspicion. It turned out he had a 5" blunt knife to cut up carrots for his pet rabbit and that his mother had washed the apron for him earlier.

164. Edward Quinn

He was born in 1853 and was a 35 year old labourer. He was arrested near Woolwich on 17th September 1888 after being found in the street covered in blood. It turned out that he had fallen over when drunk and had cut both his hands and face. No suspect here.

165. William McGrath

Born 1838 and died 1918.

He was an Irish-American watercolour painter named in the Chief Constable's Special Branch Register as: a suspicious Irishman at 57 Bedford gardens and that he is said to be connected to the Whitechapel murders. He was in London in 1888 and sailed home from Liverpool to New York on the ship Egypt, arriving on 22nd December. Perhaps there is a connection with Sickert here, did they share the same lodgings at one point?

166. Hendrik De Jong

He was mentioned in the Atlanta Constitution Georgia, U.S.A. in an article on 3rd November 1893. An alleged murderer in prison in Amsterdam could lure young women to be with him and follow him from place to place. Several of these women have disappeared. Was he in Whitechapel in 1888?

167. Joseph Lis—a.k.a Joseph Silver, Joe Eligmann, James Smith and Joseph Schmidt.

Became a pimp in South Africa and was very widely travelled. See suspect 30.

168. Ameer Ben Ali

From the Middletown Daily Times, New York, U.S.A. 24TH June 1891. The paper stated that the trial of Ameer Ben Ali, known as Frenchy and Jack the Ripper had begun. Also in an article in the Trenton Times, New Jersey, USA dated 12th September 1894 they referred to this suspect as a Syrian who was convicted as Jack the Ripper in New York and had been the victim of improper expert testimony. According to a Mr. Ewell you cannot tell the difference between Human blood and that of any other mammal through a microscope.

169. Antonio Guereo

A newspaper report from the Fresno Weekly Republican(California, U.S.A.) dated the 19th December 1890, stated that Antonio Guereo, alias Charley Ueroy, the "Jack the Ripper" of Mexico was convicted of eight murders and 14 rapes. He was sentenced to death.

170. Alfred Gamble

Gamble, aged 15, murdered children in Boston. He was described to have had a ripper style monomania. Unfortunately he was 15 in 1895 which would have made him eight years old at the time of the Whitechapel murders.

171. Arthur Williams

He made a rambling statement to Chiswick police after the double murders of 30th September 1888, in which he stated he knew who the Ripper was. Unfortunately he was drunk and possibly a lunatic. Coincidentally Arthur Williams was a pseudonym employed, from time to time, by Frederick Bailey Deeming, who became a Ripper suspect in 1892.

172. Benjamin Dunnell

Dunnell was sent for trial by Newcastle magistrates for attempting to murder Margaret Cooper, with whom he had cohabited. Earlier he had said to the woman "I will play the Whitechapel murder on you next time I see you". This was on the 13th October 1888 as reported in the Morning Advertiser (London) on the 14th October. The real Ripper would not have failed.

173. Dick Edwards

As reported in the Trenton Times, New Jersey, U.S.A. The article appearing on the 25th November 1893. A Texas murder, on trial for killing three women, is believed to be a fiend of the Jack the Ripper order. Association of style would explain this suspect. I also presume the word order here means pattern and not (Heaven forbid) a club.

174. Dr. Kudelko

As reported in the Indiana Democrat, Pennsylvania, U.S.A. on the 30th April 1890 a Dr. Kudelko, a surgeon in a hospital in Berlin, was arrested on suspicion of murdering the wife of a tailor from Benthen, on the Polish frontier. The abdomen had been split open, skilfully, from the navel down with the lower intestines spilling out. There were also other injuries not reported. It was also stated that the injuries were similar to those inflicted by Jack the Ripper. We need to know more about the injuries not reported at the time to assess if the M.O. is similar. Until that evidence is found, or made available I can give no further analysis.

175. Woolf (e) Abrahams

Brother in law of Kosminski. Aged 30, born in Russia and a master tailor. Suspect by association with the mentally ill Kosminski?

176. Morris (L. Cohen?) Lubuowski

Second brother in law of Kosminski. Aged 33, born in Poland and a boot laster. Later, in 1901, a greengrocer. Also a suspect, only by association with the mentally ill Kosminski?

177. William Wallace Brodie

Born circa 1856.

This suspect was convicted of larceny in a boarding house and in May 1877 was sentenced to fourteen years in gaol.

According to the Times newspaper (in an article published on the 7th of August 1889) he was released on licence, after serving eleven years, in August 1888. He sailed from Southampton to Kimberley South Africa on the 6th of September 1888, where he spent roughly ten months at the Sultfontein mine. He confessed to all the Whitechapel murders while in a drunken stupor in 1889.

Scotland Yard showed that he was, in fact, in S.Africa between 6th Sept 1888 and 15th July 1889.

He did, however, also confess to the murder of Alice McKenzie, even though he was, according to at least one witness, in a drunken stupor that day.

There is not much to say about this suspect except that alcoholics do have delusions which may appear very real to the person, having them, at the time.

178. Jack the myth

In a book (1933) by A.P. Wolf, it is suggested that Stride was murdered by her lover, Michael Kidney and that the rest of the victims were killed by Thomas Cutbush. Not much evidence, however, is furnished in support of these two incorporated hypotheses.

179. The lodger theory

A reporter heard an odd story that he thought could have been connected, in some way, with the murders. He got wind of the story just after the double murder. A man living not far from the British museum stated that in a room above his there was an American lodging who claimed to be a doctor, however, he did not seem to be well off although he always paid his rent on time. He was described as looking more like a 'ruffian' than a doctor. He never appears to do any work and seems to walk in a silent manner—for no one ever hears him come in. The suggestion is that he has something over his shoes to allow him to do this(compare the rubber sole shoe covers used by Joseph Barnett so as not to slip in fish oils in Billingsgate fish market). Now and again he disappears for a while and since he went out on Saturday he has not been back since. Compare the story of Tumblety, the blood stained cuffs and him disappearing after someone noticed them.

180. The Malay cook

From the Atchison Daily Globe Kansas, U.S.A. 19th November 1888. A coincidence between the Austin, Texas and Whitechapel woman murders was reported. An assassin killed eight women in

1885 in Austin, Texas. A Malay cook calling himself Maurice had been employed at the Pearl House Hotel in 1885 and that he left in 1886. All except three of the victims resided in the immediate neighbourhood of the Pearl House at the time he worked there. The women were hacked to death with an axe (one of the Ripper victims had axe wounds on her leg) and then they were sexually assaulted, possibly after death. The assertion is that he fled by steam ship to England to start a new life, lie low for a while and then start again.

181. Eppstein

Turkish priest or a grocer of 106 Suffolk Street? Are these two distinct characters or two different individuals or one witness and the other a suspect?

182. Alva Force

A robber reported in the Pennsylvania Grit, was known as Jack the Ripper. Little else, however, can be found linking him with the awful crimes in Whitechapel.

183. John Alexander Fitzmaurice

The Leadville Daily and Evening Chronicle in Colorado, U.S.A. dated the 11th of April 1889 recorded the case of a man who appeared before the authorities in Wicklow stated that he was a native of Cardiff and that his correct name was Jack the Ripper. He put this in writing and signed the document but when taken before a magistrate later he denied the statement. He then proceeded to admit to only one murder of Mary Jane Wheeler in 1888. Irish detectives then travelled to London to investigate the story from a man who appears well educated and appears to be financially well off.

184. Alaska

A sailor called George M. Dodge told the story of how he arrived in London from China aboard the steamship Glenorchy and met a Malay cook called Alaska. He related how he had been robbed of all of his money by a woman of the town and that unless he found her he would kill and mutilate every woman in Whitechapel that he could. Alaska was described as 5' 7" tall and 35 years of age. He claimed that Alaska lived in a street near East India Dock Road. Detectives made inquiries at the Glen Line Steamship company but could not find any trace of the man. Compare no.182 about a Malay cook called Maurice, the story appears similar in at least three details.

185. Walter Thomas Porriott (a.k.a.Andrew John Gibson & Charles Ernest Chadwick)

This suspects became a huge story in the Australian press after his great-great-grandson, Steve Wilson in 1997, put him forward as a suspect. His suspect status was discussed by Dusty Miller in a Ripperoo article named "new suspect; Walter Thomas Porriott". He was a convicted killer, imposter and fraudster who had no fewer than 20 wives and lived in London at the time of the Whitechapel murders after which he sailed to Australia—after which the murders stopped. He was sent to jail, for a time, for causing the death of a patient by negligence when he posed as a doctor. The sentence was for 10 years in 1940 after killing a pregnant woman (he had been posing as her gynaecologist). So he could have had a basic knowledge of anatomy and surgical skills as well. He was around 19 or 20 years old in 1888. He sailed to Australia on the 9th of November 1888, the date of the Mary Kelly murder. Later he married another woman called Kelly in the U.S.A. Folk lore suggests around the area of his grave in Australia, that here lies Jack the Ripper.

186. George James Morris

Morris was born on the 8th of February 1834, which would have made him 54 at the time of the murders. This is a little 'old' to tally with 13th of January 1882 due to a stomach disease.

He became a night watchman at the Kearley and Tonge warehouse in Mitre Square. At 1.45 a.m. on the 30th September 1888 he was sweeping some steps inside the warehouse when P.C. Edward Watkins knocked at the warehouse door saying "For God's sake mate, come to my assistance". Morris got his lamp and going out-side he asked what the matter was, Watkins replied, "there's another woman cut to pieces". Catherine Eddowes' body lay in the south-west corner of the square. Morris immediately blew his own whistle and ran along Mitre Street into Aldgate and secured the assistance of PC's Harvey and Holland to whom he related the events and all three returned to Mitre Square where Morris returned to his duties at the warehouse. Morris claimed to have been in the warehouse constantly between 11p.m. and 1.a.m. the following morning. This begs the question of what he was doing between 1 a.m. and 1.45 a.m. when the constable knocked on his warehouse door (which, by the way, was ajar.). His statements to both police and the press indicate that he would usually hear the officer on the beat in Mitre Square but heard nothing this time (not even a muffled scream?). He did, however, state in the inquest of Catherine Eddowes in answer to a question from Mr. Crawford (a solicitor acting on behalf of the police), that the warehouse door had not been ajar for more than two minutes. He could run, that was observed, and would probably have the strength to carry out the murders but would he have had the stamina? His running to elicit the extra assistance of officers was probably a learned routine gleaned from his experience as a former officer and not meant to put the police off suspecting his possible involvement (which is something to add to his defence).

One curious appendix to this suspect file is a letter dated the 19th of October 1888 written by 'an accessory' in the Metropolitan police who states: 'the crime committed in Mitre Square city and those in the district of Whitechapel were perpetrated by an ex police constable of the Metropolitan police who was dismissed from the force through certain connection with a prostitute'.

If the individual who wrote this letter had a shred of evidence in this regard, why not sign it? He died in 1907.

187. George Hutchinson

Born in Elgin, Illinois.

It was suggested by the Pall Mall Gazette in January 1889 that this person could have been Jack the Ripper. A telegram from the

Panama Star Herald outlined the facts that he had been locked away in a lunatic asylum, was handy with a knife and enjoyed visiting the asylum's slaughterhouse.

He escaped and mutilated a "disreputable woman" in Chicago in a "similar fashion to the Whitechapel murders". After several more episodes of being captured and escaping he was reported as being at large from 1886 onwards. He is not to be confused with the man of the same name who saw Mary Kelly with a suspicious looking man on the eve of her demise.

188. Olga Tchkersoff

Apparently, Tchkersoff was a Russian needlewoman. She was named by author Edwin Thomas Woodhall in a book entitled When London Walked In Terror. Aged about 24 at the time and an immigrant from Russia, she was described as dark with olive skin complexion and attractive.

She came to England on the 22nd of February 1887. Her 19 year old sister, Vera, came over too and became a prostitute. Her parents died from drink and pneumonia (mother and father in that order) and Olga despised the class of individuals who had ruined her life. Then Vera died on 28th July 1888 from septicaemia after a back street abortion. Olga started dressing in men's clothing and disappeared from the property in Spitalfields where she had once had a tailoring business.

Someone found a bloody knife of hers and destroyed this and other possible incriminating evidence (because he did not want a fellow Russian charged).

The old housekeeper who did this set sail for America two days later and dropped the knife overboard. I cannot find any evidence to support any of this. The suspect and the associated yarn are probably pure fiction.

189. George Francis (Frank) Miles

Miles was born in 1852 and died in 1891 and became a pastel artist constructing portraits of society ladies and later became a boyfriend of Oscar Wilde. He was probably bisexual as he was also engaged to be married to Gratiana Lucy Hughes and had associations with working class girls he used for his models. He was committed to an asylum near Bristol in 1887 with a general paralysis of the insane and died of exhaustion and pneumonia four years later.

An unpublished theory mentioned by Donald Rumbelow in his book The Complete Jack the Ripper. Is this Thomas Toughill's 'The Ripper Code'? It is difficult to see how this tall, ill but of athletic build (Jack the ripper was medium height and thick set) resident patient at a Bristol asylum, at the time, could have visited London, carried out the murders and sneaked back into the asylum at Brislington. Also the security there was good as several authors and researchers have elucidated e.g. Molly Whittington-Egan. Same suspect as 149.

190. The Rev. Samuel Augustus Barnett

A suspect proposed in 2006 by J. Michael Straczynski. He was born in 1844 and died in 1913. He worked in the Whitechapel area and may have known two of the victims. He also wrote letters to newspapers urging changes to social conditions in the area which he thought could be made. However I can find no reason for suspecting this individual at all.

191. William Harvey Druitt

Born 1856. Died 1909.

Druitt was the brother of Montague John Druitt and was proposed as a suspect by Andrew Holloway in 1990. I cannot find any evidence against this suspect.

192. John Kelly

He was a witness at Catherine Eddowes' funeral and was her lover. He was put forward as a possible suspect in the work Jack the Ripper: the Whitechapel Murderer. He was a fruit salesperson and jobbing porter. Suggested by Jonas, a conman, as a suspect in the murders.

193. Manuel Cruz Xavier

Xavier was born in 1851, (approximate date of birth) and was a Portuguese cattleman who has been suggested as the killer of Mary Jane Kelly by E.K. Larkins. Edward Larkins was a clerk who shared a theory about Jack the Ripper with the police (Scotland Yard) on November the 13th 1888. It implicated Antoni Pricha but this suspect turned out to have an alibi for the time of the Kelly murder. Larkins then suggested that a group of Portuguese sailors, Manuel Cruz Xavier, Jose Laurenco, Joao de Souza Machado and Joachim de Rocha committed the series of murders together. This theory too was investigated by the police and was shown to have no basis in fact.

194. A Polish Jew

A Polish Jew who frequented a Christian home in Finsbury square was reported to the police as having told an American-German medical student (named Julius I Lowenheim) that after he had contracted syphilis from a prostitute he wished to kill the person concerned and that he had a grudge against prostitutes. Little else is currently known about this suspect.

195. George Netting

Netting was supposed to have served with the Metropolitan Police in 1888 and was sacked because of regular bouts of drunken behaviour. Inquiries were made of him after Mary Ann Austin was murdered in 1901 because the last man seen with her was described as 40 years of age, with black hair, 5' 10" in height and with a cataract covering one eye. It is not known if police arrested him.

Another story connected with this character is that he had taken up lodging with his wife Mabel at 36 May street and had acted in a violent manner towards the landlady Mrs. Clarke and when his wife mentioned the murder of Austin he said "shut your bloody mouth or that will be the end of you if you are not careful". However the 1901 census details his age as 33. If so he would have been 20 at the time of the Whitechapel murders and as such would have been too young, at the time, to fit all descriptions of the Ripper.

196. John Barlas

Born 1860. Died1914.

This suspect was identified by David A. Green from a news-paper unnamed suspect and from other sources. Apparently he was a poet and was educated at Merchant Taylors' school and New College Oxford University. He was another friend of Oscar Wilde who has been suggested as a suspect (see suspect 193). Although he was wealthy from independent means he was living in squalor in 1888 with a prostitute at Hercules Buildings, Lambeth Road.

Periods of insanity followed a blow from a policeman's trun-cheon at a socialist demonstration in 1886 (being a socialist poet he was there supporting the demonstration).

Green went on to describe him as potentially violent, a lunatic and that he had been incarcerated in various asylums from 1892. At the time of the Ripper spree he was reported to have been taking regular night walks in London and was consorting with various prostitutes. Violence and madness do not equate with a series of murders using a knife. I therefore do not regard this candidate as a serious one.

197. John Murphy

Murphy was suggested as a suspect by C.J. Morley. I can find one John Murphy in the 1891 census residing at 19 Buck's Row. He was a 34 year old railway porter and was born in Bishopsgate. He was married to Johanna Murphy and they had four children, two boys and two girls. I have yet to ascertain why he was regarded as a suspect.

198. Dr. Leonard Booker Thornton (Len)

Born 1859 Died 1935.

This was a suspect who was investigated by the police in 1888 after the Mary Kelly murder and was even followed by plain clothed officers for a time. The details of this suspect were made public in 2006(in a Daily Mail article on the 2nd of December). He used his wages from transporting sick horses from a blacksmith's to the knacker's yard to fund his education at the London Hospital where he qualified as a chemist and druggist. He was an atheist and married a Catholic who became concerned when she noticed his bloodstained clothes several times after he came home from work. He alleged it was due to the nature of his work. However he made a slightly cryptic deathbed confession to a granddaughter saying 'if you knew what I have done. . . .' Later the granddaughter became convinced that he had been Jack the Ripper. A brother of the granddaughter, Michael Thornton revived this interest in the possible guilt of his grandfather. He stated that he remembered that his grandfather had a ginger moustache (link to the carroty moustache suggestions throughout Ripper folk lore).

199. Joseph Barnett

Joe came into the world on the 25th May 1858 in Whitechapel born to an Irish couple John and Catherine Barnett. He was raised, first of all in 4 Hairbrain Court, and after that in 2 Cartwright Street, less than a mile from the heart of Whitechapel.

His father died in 1864 from pleurisy when Joe was only the tender age of six. Shortly after this his mother deserted the family home. No one seems to be able to ascertain why and the eldest son Dennis took over as head of the family.

In 1869 Dennis met a local girl and moved out. Two years later the family moved a mile further north to Great Pearl Street, a street with a bad reputation in the East End. Another brother Daniel and his sister Catherine helped in raising Joe after this in difficult circumstances and made sure he got to school. He was academically a little above average at school and was able to read and write. Then on the 1st of July 1878, together with his brothers Denis and John, Joe received his market porter's licence. He was victim Mary Kelly's lover from the 8th April 1887 (when they met near his place of work at Billingsgate fish market) to the 30th October 1888, when they argued and separated (he moved to a lodging house in New Street adjacent to Bishopsgate police station) after he had lost his job and she returned to prostitution to make ends meet.

Another reason for the separation was Mary putting up another prostitute and after several days of three people together in such a small room they argued. However, he knew that she was a prostitute before they met.

Later on he lived as man and wife with Louisa, had no children and both died in November 1926 at 106 Red Lion Street, Shadwell, London. See conclusion for many further details and a full analysis. This section is highlighted too as I regard Barnett as the best suspect of all those named over the past 127 years.

He was first named as a suspect by author Bruce Paley. Also in a work of fiction, author Mark Andrews suggests, independently of Paley in a work called The Return of Jack The Ripper (1977) that it could have been Barnett.

Another Joe Barnett lived in Dorset Street at the same time born 1860 and died 1927, he played no part in the events.

Chapter 8

Conclusion

This is a special section as all the other suspects were easy to dismiss as being Jack the Ripper but the more I tried to eliminate Joe Barnett the more he fitted the pattern of Jack the Ripper.

So much data suggests that the murderer was Joseph Barnett, and since I have found much more circumstantial evidence against him than any other suspect here is a special section listing facts, conjecture on my part and quoted source material which seems to support the hypothesis that he was, out of all the suspects, Jack the Ripper. Dr. Bond who put together the first psychological-type profile of the killer suggested that he was a strong individual to have overpowered so many women with little sound having been detected and having the ability to inflict such deep knife wounds. This would fit in with him having been a market porter; there were not many weak market porters out there.

The fact that the Ripper was never caught and the various locations where the corpses were found imply that he had a superb local geographical knowledge as did Barnett.

Bardsley points out that his inactivity from Monday through to Thursday suggests he had regular employment (e.g. fish porter and later costermonger). After Poly Nichol's murder in Bucks Row, blood drops pointed west, towards Dorset Street one of at least two places he resided at during the killing spree.

The Daily Telegraph reported on the 13th of November 1888 that Barnett was on his way to see Kelly on the morning of the murder to give her three pence. It is known that Caucasian male serial killers kill Caucasian victims and Barnett was a white male.

One of the traits of an organized serial killer is that they had a relationship with at least one of their victims. Barnett, it is worth pointing out, was the live in boyfriend (off and on) of the last victim. (The majority of people who are murdered know their killer).

He also worked in Billingsgate fish market and could use a knife, a long bladed one with some skill. Even if only a porter, there is no doubt he would have regularly seen fish gutted and could take and return knives at will if he wanted to, or took home fish for Mary (her last meal was fish and potatoes) and cut them up there. If regular in this habit then he would have been used to cutting up fish, seeing what their entrails looked like and cutting in general. He wore rubber soled shoe covers so as to prevent slipping in the fish oils, explaining the fact that footfalls were hardly ever heard near the crime scenes. He had a good excuse for being out late at night when he had his job.

He had told his ex-girlfriend not to go in for prostitution or she would end up dead like the others. This was after discussing Martha Tabram's death with her, whilst showing her a copy of a newspaper cutting with details of the murder, (although she did ask him to read the details to her according to Barnett's statement).

He also had a key to her apartment, even though he claimed he had lost it, which would explain the locked door and left his clay tobacco pipe there on the mantelpiece (possibly when visiting on the previous evening at 7.45 p.m.).

He was both arrested and released at the time in connection with the murders, obviously being a chief suspect at the time. As Dr. Fred Walker has pointed out he was one of only two people who could have had a key. The other, being the landlord, having an alibi and this also provides an explanation of why Kelly's door had to be smashed in to gain access after the murder.

He had lost his job and an ex-boyfriend was bringing her money too, so jealousy could have played a role. Professor Laurence Alison, a forensic psychologist at Liverpool University believes a working class local suspect like Robert Mann (suspect 31) or Joe Barnett (my suggestion) is the closest psychological fit rather than the traditional view of an upper class killer stalking the streets of London in a cape and top hat.

Joseph Barnett from a contemporary sketch had a downturned moustache and wore a bowler hat and the sketch the press issued at the time had no moustache but was otherwise quite similar. Experts at New Scotland Yard (in the Violent Crime Directorate e.g. Laura Richards, who is a behavioural analyst and employed the combination of modern criminology and psychological profiling) produced a constructed face very similar with a downturned moustache publicised in the Daily Telegraph as an E-fit portrait (photo-fit style picture) on the 20.11.06.

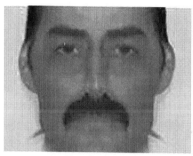

Compare this to Joseph Barnett.

In one of the letters Jack the Ripper wrote to the central press agency. He claims he drained off some blood into a ginger beer bottle but it congealed into a glue-like substance before he could use it as ink. So he used red ink instead (did he wash his hands before he posted the Dear Boss and two other letters in Miller's court?).

In Joseph Barnett's abode (13 Miller's court) there were ginger beer bottles, found by the police on November the 9th. A small point, perhaps when you consider how common ginger beer bottles were in London at that time, but it is another pointer to the character and may well serve as extra evidence towards his identity as Jack the Ripper.

The heart was taken (with care) from his-ex girlfriend, the last victim. Dr Phillips examined the remains and found Pericardium was empty, this was recently ratified by Scotland Yard who found the original document. 'I told you I would steal your heart' is suggested by this action, indicating both rage (shown on her body in the end by the violence) and intense love (took her heart out carefully and away with him) together.

Kelly after all did not give him all her love. That is how he could have viewed the situation.

He was known to be violent and had no satisfactory alibi. After Eddowes murder the killer washed his hands in a sink at Dorset Street, did Barnett live there? A girl and her mother at Leytonstone cemetery noticed, during the Mary Kelly funeral Joseph Barnett stay behind and when he thought he was alone he parted the boards above the coffin and spat several times into the grave. They were too frightened at the time to report this odd behaviour and felt that he could follow them and harm them, in some way, if they did so.

At Billingsgate fish marked he was known as John and sometimes as Jack. In the area of Dorset street, the Britannia pub and the Ten Bells pub off Commercial road were known by all the victims as well as Joe Barnett. He used to go looking for Kelly and took time off work to do so, and was seen arguing, with her, about her prostitution.

After Tabram's murder Kelly became reluctant to go out. How much more afraid would she be if the next murder appeared and was more horrific and headline grabbing still?

He had known about the secret sliding (spring loaded) bolt using the broken window (which Kelly broke in a drunken state whilst having an argument with Barnett over the suggestion that she was letting a prostitute share their lodgings, the same woman who was in her flat earlier on the evening of her murder perhaps) for access. Even the landlord's assistant did not know about that one, when he broke the door down.

According to the Penny Illustrated Paper in an article dated 17th Nov 1888 it was a catch lock and the door had been slammed shut, so why not put a hand through the broken window pane and open it again? The door must have been locked by a key. Presumably he still had a key to her apartment, so reaching in through one of the two broken windows (round the corner to the left of the door) and locking the door from the inside at the end of the crime (with her heart in a grease proof bag in his pocket) he left. There were two windows to the flat, the other being almost diagonally opposite the fire with Maria Harvey's coat as a curtain.

He told the police that the key was lost and both Kelly and himself had to use the bolt. He could have lied on this point wanting more control or to use it for the final act leaving a flat difficult to gain access to after he had made his getaway. Objects, knives et cetera, can be hidden under floorboards in cheap lodgings and clothes can be changed or burned in the grate, (hence the intense fire) and hands washed. I am not surprised the police found no blood stains on him or his clothes and his clothes were held back by the police for examination for this reason.

No bloody clothing was found at Barnett's lodgings, however he did have plenty of time to dispose of such items.

A further point on that matter is: if you have worked around smelly fish oils you would become very adept at scrubbing up after work and keep that skill for life (job or no job). A witness saw a man in the street change out of engineering overalls. Could Barnett have stolen/found or borrowed and used then burned such overalls?

In the inquest it was stated that "Witness spoke with a stutter, and evidently laboured under great emotion". This indicates echolalia or stress or both. Inspector Abberline questioned him for four hours after the Kelly murder and his clothes were examined for blood stains. He was released without charge.

However, as author Dr. Frederick Walker has stated the police, after a report was leaked to the press, that the Miller's court murder was a "copycat" murder with jealousy as the motive, still suspected Barnett.

Joseph Barnet also collected newspaper cuttings about each Ripper murder. These were left behind and passed on to a retired policeman many years later by a relative of Barnett's. According to the F.B.I. psychological profile (or criminal identification analysis as it seems to be known these days), in his childhood there should have been either an absent father or a passive father figure; Joseph's father died when he was six. It also suggests that he had some kind of physical defect which would be a source of a great deal of frustration and anger; he repeated the last words spoken to him i.e. had a speech impediment.

John Pizer, the original suspect frequented Dorset Street where he knew a man called Joe who had been intimidating witnesses—was this Barnett?

The Lusk letter is written in an Irish dialect and Joseph Barnett was Irish. Annie Chapman was found laying next to half an envelope his accommodation address consistent with the initials on the remainder of the envelope. M, Sp and 2. (presumably: Miller's court Spitalfields, 26 Dorset Street).

Walter Dew tailed the killer towards Spitalfields market. After Eddowes was murdered he fled north from Mitre square and washed in the sink in Millers court 26, Dorset Street—the same place where he later killed Kelly.

All ripper victims lived within two blocks of Dorset Street. Four of them live in Dorset Street itself. The approximate geographical centre of all the murders was Millers court. With my 'as the crow flies' analysis two foci were produced suggesting that the killer changed his address during the spree (Barnett did this). Barnett informed the authorities that on the night of the Mary Kelly murder he was playing whist until 12.30 a.m. at Buller's lodging house in New Street after which he went to bed. New Street is four minutes walk from Millers court. Playing whist was not his usual social avocation and it poses the question was it an arranged alibi, on his part i.e. that everyone assumed he was in bed instead of preparing and planning? This does not make sense as an alibi as she may have been killed between 8.30 and 10.30 a.m. anyway.

Mary Kelly was found lying on the right hand side of the bed indicating, together with most of her clothes folded on the chair, that it was someone she was comfortable with (his clay pipe on the mantelpiece also suggests her trust or his habit & left there recently). Kelly never took her clients back to her room, for fear of the Ripper or of Barnett. In his statement to the police (on the 9th of November 1888) he claims he took her from the streets (indicating his fervent wish she would not go back to her old ways of prostitution).

Two more clay pipes were found in the warm embers of the fire grate. Although the two windows should have shed enough light on the bed opposite, at 10 a.m., the coat and the muslin curtain, for privacy, were kept there, so a fire may well have been needed to throw additional light on proceedings. Smouldering clothes can be stoked up to a proper fire with newspapers (which we know Barnett bought on a regular basis), assisted by the draft through the broken windows. Did he smoke (a two pipe problem or three if you include one on the mantelpiece) while carrying out these atrocities?

Remains of female clothes were found in the grate, of course one way of putting the police off the scent that anything else important was burned is to have thrown some of her (or Harvey's) clothes on the fire after your own have been burned. If that was a clever afterthought then the fire may have been dwindling in intensity by then so some articles did not have time to burn before the fire went out, especially if the clothing was twisted, as some have reported, then they would have had a smaller surface area and as such would be very much more difficult to burn. Barnett was no scientist. Or were the clothes twisted to rinse out excess water, after soaking them, before being placed on the fire to bring it to a halt, again to divert attention elsewhere?

A clay pipe holds a small volume of tobacco; three could have been smoked in one hour from 2 to 3 a.m. or 9 to 10 a.m. (depending on the actual time of death). The fact that he was very nervous when being interviewed by the police as well as Kelly who was the centre of his life having been eliminated, at that time, explains why the killings stopped plus the suggestion that a four hour grilling by Abberline may have put him off any similar crime in the future (he was very nervous during the four hour questioning session).

What started the murders is also an interesting question; Robert Ressler, a former FBI agent suggested that "the initial murderous impulse is often triggered by some sort of pre-crime stress, such as the loss of a job . . ." In July 1888, a month before the first murder, Barnett lost his license as a fish porter and how much stress is involved in loss of a job and income together with relationship problems?

Recently a Mr. Foster (knowing his house was going to be taken as payment for loan debts after his business failed) killed his horses, dogs, wife daughter and himself. He treated his wife as a chattel (why not Barnett too?). It may have felt, one he had lost his soul mate to prostitution, two he had lost his job and the means to support himself and Kelly and three, an ex-boyfriend was reappearing on the scene with money (the means he could not provide). Therefore the solution was to remove the problem and keep her heart.

Jack the ripper strangled then cut the victims' throats. No torture, just mutilation after. What kind of serial killer wants to minimise the pain of his victims?

In 'the serial killers' by Colin Wilson and Donald Seaman (1990) they state that FBI analysts at Quantico frequently encounter serial killers who display 'mixed' disorganised and organised characteristics. This would appear to apply to Barnett leaving bodies in the open then sending letters to the press trying to involve himself in the investigation. His general M.O. suggests a serial killer who is both in love and hates prostitution at the same time (fitting Barnett again).

Catherine Eddowes claimed, two days before she was murdered, that she knew the Ripper's name. Joe Barnett seems to be the only one of the 200 Ripper suspects she could have known.

At one time Catherine Eddowes had lived in adjoining rooms to Mary Ann Kelly and they all, including Annie Chapman frequented the Britannia pub. Witnesses stated that Jack the Ripper wore a decent suit, as did Barnett in court. They also stated that he was approximately 30 years old, stout, 5' 7" tall and had a light moustache and had a deerstalker hat. This description matches Joseph Barnett closely.

A witness, Caroline Maxwell talked to Mary Kelly at approximately 9 a.m. and shortly after saw her talking to a man who looked like a market porter just before 10 a.m.

Joe Barnett was the only suspect who had been a market porter. He was noted to have been drunk at the inquest. Was this his way of mourning or something else (trying to obliterate what he had done perhaps?).

According to an FBI analysis of serial killers, disfigurement of the face of a victim (which the Ripper carried out in various forms) often means the killer knew the victim, suggesting Joseph Barnett. Also serial killers often follow press reports of the crimes, as did Joe Barnett.

A nun (roughly forty years of age) working at the Providence Row Women's Refuge opposite the pub where both Chapman and Kelly regularly met, stated, at the time of the Whitechapel murders, ' if it had not been for the Kelly woman, none of the murders would have happened'.

The author Donald Rumbelow has suggested Kelly quarrelled with Barnett over sexual inadequacies too, which could have pushed him over the edge (especially if it involved taunting because as a prostitute she may have had a large sexual appetite and he may not have had). This is an interesting point as Barnett lived on until he was 68 and never had any children (as far as I can ascertain).

Recent genealogical evidence published in Ripperana suggests that Ann was Mary Kelly's real name and not an alias. Only Joe Barnett would have known that (all the victims had combinations of Mary Ann or Annie).

There was both a tap and bin outside Kelly's apartment and Barnett would know that well. Robert Ressler (ex-FBI serial killer authority) suggests that her ears and nose were placed on a severed breast (not according to the coroner's report) in the form of a mockery of the face as one last reminder of Mary (partially regretting the series of crimes culminating in the removal of his troublesome soul mate already?).

Another report, from the inquest, places one breast next to the right foot and the other under the head next to the uterus and kidney. The Daily News in an article dated 10th November 1888 states that both breasts were placed on the table. Unfortunately the press reports were wrong. They were two piles of abdominal and thigh flesh.

He also suggested that these were disorganised crimes from a person belonging to the same social class as the victim (J.B. again).

Also thrusting a knife in was a replacement for sex (regressive necrophilia) which he had been poor at according to Kelly.

On the 19th of November 1888 the Wheeling Register, an American newspaper, ran the following story.

'I saw ... Joe Barnett ... he ... begged for money to bury his poor dear, and wanted it understood that he had a heart as well as the men with black coats on.'

Does this mean I actually care about her or does having 'a heart as well' suggest yes, the one I removed from her body (or both meanings)?

As author Bruce Paley has stated, Joseph Barnett's height, colouring and moustache match P.C. Smith's description of the man seen with Stride before her murder in Dutfield's yard. It also accurately fits Joseph Lawende's description of the gentleman seen with Eddowes before her murder in Mitre square.

Caroline Maxwell, the wife of a lodging house deputy from Dorset street, claimed to have seen Kelly at 8.45 a.m. talking to a man who looked like a market porter. The Herts. and Cambs. Reporter of 16.11.1888 named him as Joe Barnet (with one letter t). The Bristol Mercury (12.10.1888) stated that:

"seeing that it was contrary to Kelly's custom to take strangers to her room, it is believed that her destroyer offered some exceptional inducement".

This could have been financial from a stranger or Joe Barnett again.

Doctor Thomas Bond in his notes on Kelly's death stated that:

"In the Dorset street case the corner of the sheet to the right of the woman's head was much cut and saturated with blood, indicating that the face may have been covered with the sheet at the time of the attack".

This might suggest that the murderer could not bear to look at her face while attacking it (only after the crime constructing the false face); perhaps more evidence that the killer could have been Joseph Barnett? The act of placing the uterus and breast under Kelly's head indicates that he was making the statement that your head ruled your sexual areas and not your heart as it should have been. His pipe on the mantelpiece indicates that he called round that evening and since nicotine is an addiction he may well have left it there knowing he would be back shortly.

Joseph Barnett was blind drunk at the inquest (according to at least one witness). There are two interpretations of this behaviour (since in public appearances he had been well presented and respectful until then). First, this could have been his way of coping with a tragic event in his life. Second it could demonstrate that to him it was over now (the killing spree centred round Kelly) and that he wanted to block it out and later start a fresh life which he could control. It has been proposed that the Kelly murder does not fit the pattern of the other four and that someone else killed her. However with the body being indoors and much more time available to the killer to carry out the mutilations (perhaps two hours from 8.30 to 10.30 a.m.) it may simply be the same M.O. carried to completion and all serial killers become more and more daring as they proceed with their overall planned murder spree. So it may well only differ in the intensity and not the identity of the murderer. Again this fits Barnett who could now take command, with no insulting jibes from Kelly in one of her regular drunken states.

On the 30th October Elizabeth Prater, Kelly's neighbour, heard her arguing with Barnett. This argument could have been the trigger for him to perform the double event that night (Liz Stride & Catherine Eddowes). The fact that Kelly's injuries were so much worse than the other victims may have been because the killer had a personal relationship with her. The fact that the killer cut open and left on display the other victims without torture and without sex indicates that he was sending a forceful message. Uteri were removed from earlier victims because these were the instruments aiding their prostitution that which he despised. Her eyes, however, were left intact, suggesting now she will look up to me. Now at last he has the control to the end. She would not stop her ways, something he tried so hard to force her to do, this time he had the final word returning, literally, her heart to him in one, ultimate, frenzied and bloody act.

The motive was love fused with jealousy. The means were his geographical knowledge and ability with a knife and the ability to scrub up efficiently, burn clothes et cetera. And as for the opportunity he knew the prostitutes (in the pubs and through Kelly and her female associates) and had the time at night (with or without his job) to enact his crimes during unsocial hours, except for the Kelly murder which was totally on home territory.

This is a contemporary sketch of Joseph Barnett ex-fish porter and orange seller who may have sent the letters and had ginger beer bottles to hand with possibly the original intention to write one of the letters in blood but it congealed in a ginger beer bottle and he used red ink instead. He fits the portrait profiles released by the press at the time and the general description of the three reliable witnesses. His appearance also fits the 2006 e-profile compiled by Scotland Yard.

It is a pity that no photograph of Barnett seems to exist. Several people also described the hat he wore as being similar to that of a man seen in the area talking to unfortunates around that time. Well-presented and stout are descriptions that keep appearing in newspaper and other reports which again fit the sartorial and general appearance sections of the profile. He came across as one who was dressed as a porter (be it fish or fruit).

The Joseph Barnett who was a fish porter is the person, who every time I research Jack the Ripper suspects I am always forced return to. Could he have been the Ripper? It remains an open question as the Ripper might not be in any suspect list yet and may remain anonymous. However with so much circumstantial evidence together with motive, means and ample opportunity my hypothesis is (until it can be falsified) that he is guilty as charged.

The title of this book was originally JTR 200:1, this suggests 200 suspects so if you wish, to make the case complete there was no.200. Francis Spurzheim Craig the ex-husband of Elizabeth Weston-Davies (Mary Kelly). Dr.Wynne Weston-Davies, in an excellent book called The Real Mary Kelly, has been granted leave to have Kelly's remains exhumed & it's DNA tested to prove her real name. He also claims her ex-husband, a court reporter Craig, was the Ripper. However he was mentally ill and the Ripper was probably not. Furthermore he cut his own neck 15 years later after the last murder with a razor in a half-hearted way (it took him three days to expire), not at all Ripper-like. So I still think there is more evidence against Barnett as the Ripper.

Acknowledgements

Morning Advertiser article 4.9.1888—P.C. Mizen's account of Charles Cross and his activities (but called him George Cross for some reason.).

Morning Advertiser (London) article dated 26.9.1888 on Charles Ludwig.

ABC T.V. programme Catalyst—30.03.2006 analysis of gum / saliva under ripper letter stamp.

Morning Advertiser article 14.10.1888—report on Ben Dunnell threat.

Atchison Daily Globe, Kansas, U.S.A. 19.11.1888—Malay cook information.

Accessory letter from Metropolitan police file—dated 19.10. 1888

The Bristol Mercury article dated 12.10. 1888 on Mary Kelly and boarders.

The confessions of Aleister Crowley Bantam ed. March 1971 interesting only for one page 755 where he describes Cremers picking the lock of a box of seven white evening dress ties all stiff and black with clotted blood, the box having its place under the bed of Roslyn D'Oynston Stephenson.

CSI Las Vegas T.V. series episode (2009) where the pathologist expounds the latest theory on handedness and killers.

Croyden Advertiser article on bloodhounds dated 13.10. 1888.

1891 census on-line.

Criminologist periodical (1968)—analysis of the from hell letter by C.M. MacLeod.

Dr. Dutton's Chronicles of crime—about Dr. Pedachenko.

Dorset Chronicle article dated 10.1.1889 on M.J. Druitt.

Daily News article 16.11.1888 about Collingwood H. Fenwick.

Daily News article dated 4.10.1888 on labour delegates forming a vigilance committee.

Evening News article dated 11.9.1888—L. Forbes Winslow on tracking J.T.R. and his being viewed as a suspect together with data on the elusive Wentworth Bell Smith.

Eastern Post & City Chronicle dated 27.10.1888 general information.

Echo dated 1.9.1888—on the High-Rip gang.

Fido Martin, The Crimes, detection and death of Jack The Ripper (1987).

Fort Wayne News, Indiana, U.S.A. an article dated 23.3.1903—on the trial of George Chapman.

FBI psychological profile on serial killers—from the J.T.R. Casebook website.

Fanny Drake—reported a figure similar to the description of J.T.R. on the 21.11.1888.

Fresno Weekly Republican, California, U.S.A.—dated 19.12.1890 on Antonio Guereo.

Herts. & Cambs. Reporter paper dated 16.11.1888 an article with a little miscellaneous detail on Joe Barnett.

Indiana Democrat, Pennsylvania, U.S.A., dated 30.04.1890 about suspect Dr. Kudelko.

Jack the Ripper; Anatomy of a myth. By William Beadle (Wat Tyler books, 1995)—good for data about suspect William Bury.

Jack The Ripper the final solution by Stephen Knight (revised ed. 1984 treasure press hardback.) Although Gull was not a freemason, interesting theory used for the basis of the plot in the film 'From Hell' (2001) with Jonny Deppe et al.

Jack The Ripper the mystery solved by Paul Harrison Paperback edition 1993 published by Robert Hale Ltd., interesting detail pertaining to the Goulston Street graffito but he missed the slip that Mary Kelly had been wearing and the fact that two Joe Barnetts lived in the area.

The complete Jack the Ripper by Donald Rumbelow revised ed. 2004—published by the penguin group. Superb in almost all the detail but scientific knowledge lacking in the area of egg / D.N.A. and yolk which he confused by mixing up between hen's egg and Human egg.

The Complete Jack The Ripper A to Z by Paul Begg, Martin Fido and Keith Skinner in hardback published in 2010 by John Blake Publishing Ltd. Superb all round reference book except for the date 1965 p. 520 instead of 1865.

Robert Keppel and Joseph Weis 17.03.05 internet article analysis of Washington homicides (1981-95)—implying that the signature of JTR's killings was very rare.

Karen Poulin—carried out a handwriting analysis of Dr. Pearson claiming it to be very close to the style exhibited in the agreed ripper letters to the press—on messageboards / casebook.org.

Lloyd's Weekly News—1912 article on a quote from Inspector Edmund Reid.

The Lodger 1994 by Stewart Evans & Paul Gainey (suggests Tumblety).

Leadville Daily & Evening Chronicle, Colorado, U.S.A. article dated 11.04.1889—information on suspect J.A. Fitzmaurice.

Edward Larkins—J.T.R. theory on Portuguese cattlemen, shared with the police at the time. Article dated 13.11.1888.

Mei Trow (2009)—for Robert Mann suspect information.

Mountain Democrat 01.04.1893—Frank Casellano 'Jack the Ripper in custody'.

Middletown Daily Times, N.Y. an article dated 24.06.1891 on suspect Ameer Ben Ali.

Daily Mail 02.12.2006 on Dr. L.B. Thornton (Len, as his friends knew him)—suspect details.

New York Times article dated 29.04.1892 about Deeming and his alleged confession to having been the perpetrator of most of the J.T.R. killings.

The Daily News an article dated 10.11.1888—incorrect story of the placement of Mary Kelly's breasts in her apartment after death.

Ripper Podcasts

http://www.casebook.org/podcast

Put together and fronted by Jonathan Menges, each goes on for about one hour. Good for the odd magpie scraps of useful arguments and nuggets of interesting detail, however you want to shout out, after about half an hour each time, "get on with it.", i.e. there is too much general banter to keep the interest going, is my only criticism.

Pall Mall Gazette article dated 01.10.1888—body cost pickled.

Pall Mall Gazette article dated January 1889 on George Hutchinson of Elgin, Illinois, U.S.A.

Ripperologist Magazine (1999 & 2000) articles on Jacob Hyam Levy by Mark King.

Ripperana article on Mary Kelly's name.

Robert Ressier—ex. F.B.I. authority on serial killers.

The Return of Jack the Ripper (1977) a work of fiction by Mark Andrews—suggests independently of Paley the view of Barnett (d.1926) as a main suspect.

Reynolds's Newspaper article on the Jewish vigilance committee—dated 16.09.1888.

Southern Guardian article dated 01.01.1889

On M.J. Druitt.

The Star Newspaper (London)—article dated 18.09.1888 on Jacob Isenschmid.

The Star Newspaper article dated 10.11.1888 about W.H. Eaton.

The Star Newspaper in an article dated 10.09.1888 on St. Jude's vigilance committee.

The Daily Telegraph article dated 20.11.2006—for an e-fit portrait of J.T.R. based on the most reliable witness statements, prepared by Laura Richards at Scotland Yard.

Daily Telegraph article dated 13.11.1888

The Real Mary Kelly by Dr.Wynne Weston-Davies Blink Publishers 2015.

On Joe Barnett and 3d prospective visit to M. Kelly on the day of her death.

Daily Telegraph article dated 12.09.1888 on suspect John Pizer.

Daily Telegraph article dated 06.10.1888 on suspect John Lagan.

Daily Telegraph article dated 05.10.1888 on the Lusk vigilance committee.

Trenton Times N.J., U.S.A., an article dated 12.09.1894 on the Syrian suspect Ameer Ben Ali.

Trenton Times, N.J., U.S.A., article dated 25.11.1893 on suspect Dick Edwards.

Times Newspaper in an article dated 07.08.1889—on suspect W.W. Brodie.

Tony Williams / Humphrey Price (2005).

In a book called Uncle Jack one or two interesting pieces of data are found scattered throughout.

http://www.ripperologist.biz a good internal search engine showing interesting details of back numbers and their articles.

http://www.whitechapelsociety.com.

A well-illustrated web site with good points of historical interest & description of pubs in the area frequented by the victims.

http://www.walksoflondon.co.uk/28/index.sntml.

This web site is useful for geographical, photographic and historical background.

The Wheeling Register (American Newspaper) article dated 19.11.1888—Barnett funeral arrangements and costs.

Article by Dr. F. Walker on Barnett in casebook J.T.R. some excellent points made here.

The serial killers by Colin Wilson & Donald Seaman (1990)—for one or two interesting points but errors from early newspaper reports litter the pathway to the truth.

Richard Wallace (1996) theory on T.V. Bayne & Lewis Carroll. Just like the translation of the Loch Ness monster's name into scientific binomial nomenclature then an anagram was used to show it was a hoax, so anagrams and Latin variations of names are squashed to form a theory. Good for brain exercise, but not much else.

E-book by Christopher J. Morley 2004(Jack the Ripper 150 suspects) on; casebook: Jack the Ripper hhtp://www.casebook.org/ripper-media/book-reviews/non-fiction/cjmorley/index.html

http://www.met.police.uk/history/ripper.htm

Repeats the original police suspect list, good, however, for some interesting photographs.

http://en.wikipedia.org/wiki/Jack-the-ripper

This is a good site for death certificate copies and photographs of the victims.

http://www.casebook.org

An outstanding site for a. Newspaper articles, b. pictures of suspects, c. Biographical details of suspects and d. a superb general index showing the number of pages allocated to each topic or suspect.

www.UkcensusOnline.com

St. James Gazette—article dated 13.11.1888—Barnett's inquest evidence on Mary Kelly.

Penny Illustrated Paper—article dated 17.11.1888—seems to suggest the locked door clicked shut on slamming rather than just bolted and with the knowledge that one could reach through the broken pane to move the bolt the door must have been locked as well by key.

Jack the Ripper Artwork

What follows next is a selection of artist impressions specially commissioned for this book of Jack the Ripper drawn from the most reliable witness statements. They are drawn by my sister, Helen Westfield.

147

Made in the USA
Lexington, KY
01 April 2018